MORE ADVANCE PRAISE FOR
Citizen Soldier

"Aida Donald has written a succinct and gripping life of one of our most remarkable presidents, marked in particular by an original and highly engaging portrait of Truman as a young man. Truman took more than forty years to discover his real vocation, yet left an enduring mark on the nation and the world."

—David Kaiser, author of
The Road to Dallas: The Assassination of John F. Kennedy

"*Citizen Soldier* rivetingly reveals Truman the man and what shaped him—his family and his wife, battlefield service in World War I, and entanglements with the politics of the Pendergast machine. Donald judiciously takes the measure of his presidency while recounting how the inner man coped with the burden of his momentous decisions, from the atomic bombing of Japan to the waging of war in Korea. A moving and insightful biography."

—Daniel J. Kevles, Stanley Woodward
Professor of History, Yale University

"Aida Donald has brought a keen focus back on Harry Truman the person. Not so much a policy tome, this is about the interior life of a decent, seemingly ordinary person—a kind of real life 'Mr. Smith'—finding himself drawn more and more to the center of a very messy political world. The more we recognize Truman as a common man, the more we recognize in him a bit of ourselves, the more we appreciate the way he learns and copes with choices, great and terrible, that marked an age. Donald wears her deep knowledge lightly; her portraiture is swift yet thoughtful."

—Philip Zelikow, Associate Dean for the Graduate School & White Burkett Miller Professor of History, University of Virginia

"A skillful psychobiography by an empathetic scholar."

—*Kirkus Reviews*

CITIZEN
SOLDIER

ALSO BY AIDA D. DONALD

Lion in the White House: A Life of Theodore Roosevelt

John F. Kennedy and the New Frontier (Editor)

CITIZEN SOLDIER

A LIFE OF

HARRY S. TRUMAN

Aida D. Donald

BASIC BOOKS

A MEMBER OF THE PERSEUS BOOKS GROUP

New York

Published by Basic Books,
A Member of the Perseus Books Group

Books published by Basic Books are available at special discounts
for bulk purchases in the United States by corporations, institutions,
and other organizations. For more information, please contact the
Special Markets Department at the Perseus Books Group, 2300
Chestnut Street, Suite 200, Philadelphia, PA 19103, or call (800)
810-4145, ext. 5000, or e-mail special.markets@perseusbooks.com.

Designed by Timm Bryson

Library of Congress Cataloging-in-Publication Data
Donald, Aida DiPace.
  Citizen soldier : a life of Harry S. Truman / Aida D. Donald.
    p. cm.
  Includes bibliographical references.
  ISBN 978-0-465-03120-7 (hardcover : alk. paper)—ISBN 978-0-
465-03307-2 (e-book) 1. Truman, Harry S., 1884–1972. 2. Presi-
dents—United States—Biography. 3. United States—Politics and
government—1945–1953. 4. Soldiers—United States—Biography.
I. Title.
  E814.D66 2012
  973.918092—dc23
  [B]
                                                        2012025583

10 9 8 7 6 5 4 3 2 1

For Kathleen Nichols

CONTENTS

INTRODUCTION

In May 2011, in an interview, Condoleeza Rice, recent Republican Secretary of State, stated: "Harry Truman probably is the greatest president to my mind of the post–World War II era." Dr. Rice was undoubtedly referring to Truman's putting the world back together again after the most devastating war in the modern era. Through economic and military action, he saved then revived Europe and Japan. A Soviet expert, she also must have had in mind that Truman mostly stopped the spread of communism from a powerful and dictatorial Soviet Union.

Truman's reputation was not always so high. While he received an 82 percent approval rating at the end of World War II, it sank to almost half that a year later, and fell even further during the Korean War to 23 percent. More important, when he left office he was considered a failed president, or second rate. He was not ranked with those midgets Pierce, Buchanan, Harding, Coolidge, Hoover, and a few others. But he was far below the greats. Only recently has his reputation risen to a high level, below Lincoln, Washington, Jefferson, and the two Roosevelts, to be sure, but near the nineteenth-century figure of Andrew Jackson. Time has shown the strength of character he possessed and the wisdom to govern well during many crises.

Splendid biographies by David McCullough, Alonzo Hamby, Robert J. Donovan, and Robert Ferrell have surely boosted Truman's reputation. Dozens of specialized books; documents in the Truman Library in Independence, Missouri; the opening up of hitherto-secret archives there and in Washington; and the extraordinary access to significant materials through the Internet throw light on his various endeavors and political offices to give us a deepened view of his times and life. Those of us who attempt to write a life of Truman, especially one that is short and interpretative, stand on the shoulders of all these giants and are greatly in debt to archivists' work. I am one of these immensely indebted to previous historians and keepers of records, whom I have not only come to admire but also to hold in affectionate regard.

Like other Truman biographers, I have struggled to figure out where I stand on the puzzling issues of Truman's life. I am more inclined to interpret Truman's life psychologically than other biographers of the president. In the pages that follow, I stress the powerful and opposing tugs at him by his father and mother when he was a young man, after what he called an idyllic childhood. But the family was always on the move, and his college-educated mother raised him to read, play the piano, and love music, plays, and opera. And she put up with her often-improvident husband with his many business failures. Truman left a promising life and career in a bank in Kansas City, Missouri, where he reveled in the high culture of the place, when ordered home by his father to help run the family farm. The young man was unhappy for ten years in the lonely, desperate work to make the farm prosper, with no, or little, success.

Truman ran away from the farm and its isolation and drudgery to volunteer in the army in 1917, and it became a landmark decision in his life. I stress the importance of Truman's World War I soldiering, when he was an excellent officer who molded a wild bunch of men into a fighting artillery battery that came to admire him. His initiatives under fire, outside his sector, saved others' lives, but such actions sometimes brought threats of court-martial by stiff-necked colonels, although General John J. Pershing praised his battery, as will be shown. The war made Truman the man he dreamed of becoming when a shy, bespectacled boy, who mostly played with girl cousins and learned the art of cooking and babysitting from his mother, all of which made him a "sissy" (his word).

Truman's love for and devotion to Bess Truman, from age six, is woven into the story. She was a polestar in his life, although she hardly noticed him for years, and perhaps her unavailability for so long was a challenge, as well as a safety net, to his growing manhood. The Victorian-Edwardian era, as well as the previous Romantic period, made much of men loving the unobtainable as a hedge against a known inability to connect with young women. When Harry went to Washington, Bess appears as less than the loving helpmate Truman needed. She preferred to live in Independence with her mother for half of every year, even though Harry desperately needed her during periods of turmoil in his political career. Their daughter, Mary

Margaret, called Margaret, was the object of his total affection, which she reciprocated.

The real puzzles of Truman's career were what made me want to tell his story. Although the corrupt Kansas City Pendergast political machine drew him into politics, how did he manage to stay honest in such a den of thieves? I offer a psychological interpretation to explain this phase of his life—a local politician in charge of millions of dollars for development in Jackson County, as county judge, an administrative position in Missouri. My portrait is immeasurably aided by a new reading of the memos of the once-secret Pickwick Papers in the Truman Library. Truman often had to make deals with corrupt politicians, but they made him very ill with blinding headaches and stomach problems. He hid out in hotels, and it was there he wrote the Pickwick letters/memos, named for the Kansas City hotel he chose most often as a hideaway, about his dubious political actions, and he named those who were skimming taxpayer monies. Long hidden, the Pickwick Papers have been made available only recently to biographers, but only I read them for psychological insight. Mostly they have been used to track the corruption Truman found in government and revealed in these memos and letters he kept secret. But he saved them for posterity, for they could exculpate him from charges of major fraud, while revealing the local history he was a part of. He believed in the power of truth in history.

Another puzzling problem for any Truman biographer is his use of atomic bombs against Japan. In telling the history of these events, the building of the bomb and its use, I offer new portraits of Secretary of War Henry Stimson and the builder of the bomb, the scientist J. Robert Oppenheimer. Truman weighed his options in figuring out the bomb's use, with incomplete information about how devastating it was. I don't argue that he would never have used it, just that the story is more complicated than hitherto written about, with new judgments about the characters of its intimate deciding-personnel, both scientists and policy makers.

Truman was an accidental president. I examine how he governed as chief executive, in the shadow of a Lincolnian predecessor, as big a figure as Truman was small. But I also pay a lot of attention to Truman's learning experiences back home in Missouri, as well as in Washington as a senator. He was not an inexperienced politico, as often portrayed. Mostly, the problem was that President Roosevelt told him nothing and ignored him. While Truman's Senate career is reimagined here, in light of his later prominence as head of state, it naturally lacked the depth and breadth needed to prepare him to be president, even though he had good experience as an executive in Missouri and as a leading senator. His select committee on defense spending ferreted out fraud and corruption, while being a marvel of judiciousness and success. The experience catapulted him to national prominence, even catching the attention of Roosevelt and his advisers, who picked him for vice president because he would lose the party the fewest votes in 1944.

I show how Truman tried to master the world war and domestic problems, which were incredibly severe. His learning curve took about eighteen months to put him on top of problems, too long to keep the Congress Democratic—Republicans swept into office in the 1946 elections—but better advice from new appointments like Dean Acheson helped. He also became the Harry Truman of legend by being himself, Middle America's latest populist leader, who could arouse the people to his side, and make significant decisions abroad and at home. He became a fervent New Dealer with his Fair Deal, although it was mostly scuttled amid the Korean War. The Fair Deal did not emerge full blown from his head. He mentioned a "fair deal" for people in speeches, but it was journalists who picked up the words and made it into "the Fair Deal." Truman liked that, as it followed the widely admired New Deal. So the politics of the year and a half after the war ended was a congeries of policies, with no coherence until it was shaped by a new label. He called his politics progressive liberalism. But his domestic policies had few victories. The 80th Congress, 1947–1949, was hostile. Republicans were bent on breaking the president and making the next presidential election theirs. Truman got some Social Security reforms, desegregated the army, and made some civil rights advances. But he was mostly irate and often bad-tempered toward Congress. In fact, Truman's barnyard language as a politician is noted, as the farmer overtook the usually genial and gentlemanly politico.

I take a new look at how good intentions to uphold the fledgling United Nations, intent on meeting aggression in Korea, slid into tragedy, in an Asian war that could not be won. That war took down a genuine military hero, General Douglas MacArthur, who argued that there was no substitute for victory in Korea. He would not follow Truman's orders to keep away from the Chinese border or to do anything to entice China or Russia to enter the Korean War and not to intimate, in any way, that atomic arms might be used to turn the tide when the UN forces were being overrun. Truman was bent on avoiding the use of atomic weapons or giving China or Russia any excuse to enter the war, which could set off World War III. Like Washington and Lincoln before him, he acted to maintain the constitutional imperative of the president as commander in chief. President Truman fired MacArthur.

Truman won his own term of office in an election in 1948 that no one thought he could win. No one. It was the biggest upset in the nation's political history. This is a good story in itself, retold here, and it can be claimed as a personal triumph, not one of his tired, and too-long-serving, Democratic Party. Not insignificantly, his coattails brought Democrats back into power in Washington. But these years recalled the trials of his first term, with a Cold War with the Soviet Union, the Berlin blockade, and Soviet domination of Eastern Europe. Truman operated with the notion that aggression had to be met forthrightly; Hitler's aggression had not been, and a world war was the result. With the dominoes of communism staining policy, with un-American loyalty oaths and Republican demagoguery, a new kind of America formed during these years. From the arsenal of democracy in World War II, America built a great military-industrial complex, the only superpower of the world, alert to aggressions that, it soon found out after great amounts of blood and treasure were spent, it could not block.

This short book is written for a general reader. It is a narrative, a conversation with the reader, and not freighted with notes. I am reaching out for understanding, if not for sympathy, for those whose story this is. The light and dark of Truman's life is limned. The reader can discern the shaping of his character and the tight knot of his love for his wife and family, which sustained him, and his placement of loyalty above all other sentiments, something he learned as a solder and a young politician and later got him into trouble when friends became light-fingered in his late second term and tarred Truman, unfairly, with the stench of corruption.

Truman's life is not a straight path to understanding him, but a winding trail, with bends of astonishment, discovery, and sometimes disappointment. Even in this late day, I hope I have new things to say and new ways of configuring Truman's life that will make this book welcome.

CHAPTER 1

THE WEB
OF FAMILIES

Harry Truman's earliest memory was of a happy childhood with a mother of frontier certitude and a father who could be kind or firm. Although the family's ancestral state was Kentucky, Harry was born in Lamar, Missouri, on May 8, 1884. The Trumans lived in a newly built, cabin-like, wood-frame structure, only twenty-eight by twenty feet, with six tiny rooms. It had no running water or plumbing, a pump and outhouse being the ordinary utilities. A good notion of what Harry's natal area looked like can be found in the realistic paintings of the nineteenth-century frontier artist George Caleb Bingham. A narrative of the pioneer families of Truman's ancestors forms part of Francis Parkman's stirring book *The California and Oregon Trail.* How settlers traversed the Missouri River to get from Kentucky to Missouri was the intrepid John Charles Frémont's tale. Even nature's great artist, John James Audubon, visited the area to paint birds majestic and mundane.

Harry's father, John Anderson Truman, broke with the normal way of arriving in Missouri by steamboat. He rode a horse from Kentucky to Missouri, a perilous journey. Contrary and poor, John unknowingly set a Truman pattern of contrariness, although dreaming it could be something else. John was the third of five children. Born in 1851, he was a short, five-feet four-inch, compact, strong man, with dark hair and a sunburned, brown face. He was educated in a rural school. John's family was poor when they were in Kentucky, and that was likely why they migrated to Missouri, where there were more opportunities.

In Missouri, in Jackson County, the Trumans owned 200 acres, which John helped farm. As he grew to manhood, John was known for his integrity and hard work but also for his ferocious temper when challenged about his family or business practices. To his own family, he was mostly kind, but he was stern when he needed their help to make a good living. He was thirty years old when he married Martha Young in 1881, and they moved to Lamar, Missouri. John bought her a small house for $685 (roughly $15,000 in 2012 dollars), with a big barn for his proposed livestock trading. His father sold his farm and moved in with them. They stayed only three years there, as John did not prosper.

Martha Ellen Young Truman, Harry's mother, was a year younger than John, two inches taller, slender with light blue eyes and dark hair, and an alert look. She had a round face, which Harry undoubtedly inherited. She was lively and a good dancer, most probably with anyone but serious John. Unusual for women of her generation, she graduated from college. At

FIGURE 1   Martha Ellen Young Truman and John Anderson Truman, wedding photo, December 28, 1881. *Credit:* Courtesy of the Harry S. Truman Library.

the Baptist College for Women in Lexington, Missouri, she studied music, literature, and art, which would soften the edges of her long, often hard life. She was, according to one account, "as tough as a barrel of nails," but she shaped the future president more than anyone else, and he was her favorite. His father influenced Harry, but it seemed he only emphasized those aspects of Harry's life that Martha had already imprinted, except for Harry's strong cultural streak, which was all Martha's doing.

Martha was the eighth child of Solomon and Harriet Louisa Gregg Young. Solomon had trekked from Kentucky to Jackson County, in 1841, hauled freight, led cattle drives west, and owned land in California, which he had bought from the Spanish. Years later, he sold it for $75,000, which today would equal roughly $1.25 million. He returned to Missouri and, by 1861, owned 1,300 acres of prime land. By 1869 Solomon and his formidable wife owned 2,000 acres. He had suffered from the Civil War ravages and hated Abraham Lincoln. As a farmer and businessman, he was more than exemplary within his family. When he died intestate in 1892, his wife inherited everything.

In 1887 John Truman became Solomon's partner and managed the Young farm in Grandview until 1909, when Grandmother Young died. John had already given up his first house in Lamar, after three years, and had moved to Harrisonville, in Cass County. He bought 120 acres of his own, forty of them from his father-in-law. Now, in Grandview, he would experience a new beginning, when Martha's mother left her half of the farm. But it was not unalloyed joy for John and Martha. Because she cut out her other children, the Trumans would be engaged in a battle with Martha's siblings that lasted for years, almost impoverishing them all with legal bills.

The Young house that Harry's family lived in until 1890 was a picture-book structure, white with green trim. Along with relatives and farm and house hands, it was home to some fourteen or fifteen people. It was smaller than their imposing, homestead house, which had burned down. Nevertheless, it had a kitchen, dining room, front parlor, sitting room, and two bedrooms. It had no electricity, plumbing, or running water. Harry and his brother Vivian climbed a narrow back stairway to a little bedroom with two windows, under the eaves over the dining room. Clearly, more space was given for possible socializing than for the family's comfort.

Some of Solomon's energy and hopes resided in Martha. She played the piano, and taught Harry to play before he needed more expert training. Harry got that through his teen years and until he could no longer afford music lessons. At one time, he thought he wanted to be a concert pianist. Martha bought books for Harry, whom she taught to read at age four or five. Accounts vary. They were mostly of heroes and leaders but, also, of poets and novelists. The boy became a demon reader. The kernel of Martha's existence, however, was more pioneer than dilettante. She could handle guns and was supreme in the household and as a parent while her children were growing up. Aside from Harry, there were John Vivian, always called Vivian, who was two years younger than Harry, and Mary Jane, the baby.

Martha was a beloved mother to Harry and a person of great expectations. It was on Harry, and not his brother Vivian or sister

FIGURE 2   Formal portrait of Harry Truman (age four) and his brother,
John Vivian Truman (age two), 1888. *Credit:* Thomson Studio, courtesy of
the Harry S. Truman Library.

Mary Jane, that she doted, even teaching him how to cook, keep
house, and tend to his baby sister. Martha, it was recalled, said:
"He was intended for a girl." Harry remarked in his autobiography
that he was a "sissy." He cooked breakfast for the farmhands—
oatmeal, fried eggs—and according to one farmworker, he

made the best biscuits. Harry tended Martha's vegetable garden and milked the household cow. Very early, Vivian opted for a male existence in his father's shadow, renting a farm, marrying young, and having two children, twins. From early childhood, Mary Jane was a tomboy. She never married and stayed home with her mother, who lived to be ninety-four. Harry was expected to excel not only in domestic chores but also in school. He was a good student, and it was thought he would go to college, as had his mother. In his trying to understand her teachings about helping and learning, his moral and ethical behavior came from her Methodist religion. It probably would be wise to conclude that he was a teachable child, who wanted to be helpful to gain favor, and his mother's lessons, beyond the domestic, were more or less what Methodists believed.

Harry had several memories of early childhood. One was of chasing a frog in his yard when he was two, in 1886, and thoroughly enjoying it, laughing boisterously. Around the same time, he was dropped by his confident mother from a second-floor window into the strong arms of his uncle Harrison Young, Martha's brother. Harrison was the rich bachelor, a farmer and landowner, who would play an important role in the boy's life. Harrison was a heavy-set man, six feet tall, strong and good-looking, according to Truman's autobiography. He seemed unlike the Trumans. Harry was named after Harrison, and the middle initial came from his grandfathers, Solomon Young and Anderson Shippe Truman. He did not favor either grandparent in explaining what the S stood for in his name. In fact, decades later, when the chief justice of the Supreme Court was swearing Harry in as president and called him Harry Shippe Truman, the about-to-be-president corrected him by saying his name was Harry S. Truman. Another early memory was of Harry's mother's screams when his sister, Mary Jane, was born. He was five years old.

Martha was ambitious for her children. In the summer of 1890, she moved the family to Independence so Harry and his siblings could get a good education. With a population of six thousand, Independence was a growing town, a day's ride west of Kansas City. Still a frontier town, it had only a thin layer of civilization. That is, its infrastructure was minimal, but it had pretensions. Independence was well situated to benefit from the growing American economy. The trails to the West Coast, to rich farmland in Oregon and gold in California, began there. But its history, two generations before Harry was born, was violent. A bitter war in 1838 drove out the Mormons. Then the Union Army desolated the area, at one point evicting 20,000 inhabitants from three counties, including Jackson County, the home of Independence. After the Civil War, Confederate guerrillas, led by William Quantrill, ravaged the land. The Civil War was a bitter heritage for Harry, whose mother never forgave the Union Army. When as a young man he showed up in the blue dress uniform of the state militia, he was scolded: "Harry, this is the first time since 1863 that a blue uniform has been in this house. Don't bring it here again." Dutiful Harry, crestfallen, never did.

Harry lost a year in school in 1894, when he had diphtheria, but it did not set him back and, actually, he soon advanced a grade. We have to assume that Martha was a good educational

surrogate. Harry was an avid
student. He would later recall
these earliest years as a paradise. He had plenty to eat, a little sister he adored, a pony,
hundreds of acres to roam in,
and kindly relatives who were
interested in being with him.

At first, in Independence,
the Trumans lived in a white
clapboard house. Carpenters
had built it from a plan book,
but it had extra flourishes: a
cupola and a gilded weather-
vane. Harry would listen for

FIGURE 3 Harry Truman, age thirteen,
1897. *Credit:* Harry S. Truman Library.

train whistles and watch the iron horses whiz by. He loved
trains all his life, as he loved books. Two black servants resided
with the family. Five years later, in 1895, John moved the family
to another, more fashionable, house. John was prospering in
the 1890s, in a nation suffering a depression. He was an active
Democrat, and he took sixteen-year-old Harry with him to the
Democratic National Convention in 1900 in Kansas City.
Harry's idol became William Jennings Bryan, "The Great
Commoner," who was running for president a second time,
against William McKinley. Harry was a good son, tending to
farm animals like a milk cow and weeding his mother's garden,
activities a Mama's boy engaged in, even generations later in
American farm families.

Harry went to high school after the seventh grade. There he met a brilliant student, Charles G. Ross, who would be his all-time closest friend and confidant. Ross would become his press secretary when Truman was president. Of all his characteristics, Truman held the elements of friendship—loyalty—with the greatest regard, mostly for good, but sometimes for ill, in his political career. At age fifteen, Harry, a devoted history buff, recorded his life's aim this way: "A true heart, a strong mind, and a great deal of courage and I think a man will get through the world." These few words guided him in life, although he never could have conceived that he would rise to the pinnacle in politics.

Harry also carried into these adolescent years his unrequited penchant for Bess Wallace, whom he first espied as a six-year-old in class. He always said that she was his one and only love, the love of his life, although she didn't notice him until he was in his teens and, then, very little. Harry clung to an impossible romance, impossible not only because he was not noticed but also because he was a lone youngster, with no male chums, an imposing mother, and a non-social schedule of chores, piano playing, and music lessons. Slim, bespectacled, round-faced, ultra-polite, and shy, Harry lived in a world of family and quiet thoughts. He was not a boy's boy, like Vivian. His gang consisted of girls, his sister and two cousins, Ethel and Nellie Noland, who kept in close touch with him throughout their lives. Truman's early socialization, mostly with girls and seldom with boys, switched irreversibly in his early manhood, because of his army experience. Now, he was not comfortable with women—later, he would not have them in his cabinet—and he preferred the company of men, whether in voluntary organizations or in political office. Even raucous behavior was tolerated at his army reunions, while drinking—never to excess—and card playing with male friends were his diversions. The army made him a man's man, and he was comfortable in his new persona, although rather overdramatic in its application.

A good student in high school, Harry was conscientious and well behaved. The curriculum was conservative: natural science, mathematics, the classics, rhetoric, logic, history, and English literature. He never liked science, which was a serious limitation for his later career, particularly since his most controversial decision as president involved a scientific question of profound significance. History was his favorite subject, but he had a knack for mathematics, too, which helped him when he was an artillery officer in World War I. He was a great reader on his own, boasting that he read all 3,000 books in the local library. A centrally important work in his own private library was Charles F. Horne's *Great Men and Famous Women.* Of great men, Harry most admired Alexander the Great, Hannibal, Charles Martel, Cincinnatus, and Robert E. Lee. He never mentioned the famous women and, in fact, soon after he became president, he was relieved when Frances Perkins, Franklin Delano Roosevelt's Secretary of Labor, the first and only woman to serve in a cabinet up to that time, left his cabinet. He wanted only men advisers. He read Caesar, Cicero, Plutarch, Marcus Aurelius, Ralph Waldo Emerson, and Mark Twain. He later saw some merit to Lincoln, after discounting family prejudice. His mother remained an unreconstructed Southerner, even refusing to sleep in the Lincoln Bedroom, which Truman restored from the assassinated president's office, when the White House was renovated while he was president. Harry's love of history stood him in good stead, as he referred to great men's affairs while discussing weighty issues when he was in the army, or when he was settling world problems with other leaders, including Joseph Stalin, who was impressed. Truman had a Whiggish view that progress was the story of mankind. He got his life maxim from Benjamin Franklin: "Always do right. This will gratify some people and astonish others."

Some historians compare Truman's self-education and reading to the education of his predecessor, Franklin Roosevelt, and of FDR's cousin, Theodore, who attended the elite Groton and Harvard. Of Theodore, the fragile boy with bad eyesight but an omnivorous reader, there is a resemblance, minus the disparity in wealth and broad culture. Each had an unreconstructed Southern mother. Each became an accidental president. But the parallels end there. (With FDR, there is little parallel, only a political inheritance.) Theodore made a manly body in his teens. And he was scientifically shaped at Harvard. It is doubtful that Truman knew much science, even of the atomic bomb, which he would unleash in 1945, still his most controversial decision. Truman was locked into a narrow personal and community ambience, and the Great War made him a man. Theodore Roosevelt, a quondam cowboy, also went to war, the Spanish-American War in Cuba, but he had already been in government. Where TR was cosmopolitan—he visited Europe and the Middle East as a boy with his family—and expansive, Truman was commonsense-practical with simple virtues. Each believed that men made history, however, and were not pawns of fate. They were both more Roman than Greek from their broad reading.

In his reminiscences, Truman cast a bright glow on his growing up and the lessons he took into manhood. It is doubtful that he was as inner directed and aggressive as his father. His slight physique and bad eyesight made him conciliatory. Tossed as he was between the need often to be aggressive and his chosen stance of conciliation, there would be psychic costs to him.

When he graduated from high school in 1901, Harry had a moon-shaped, pleasant face and a sharp nose. He was not muscular and was in fact a bit heavy. He wore thick glasses and was teased a lot. He fantasized about having a military career and fooled around with fencing. His poor eyesight kept him out of West Point. He wanted to go to college. Only outwardly, however, did his father seem rich enough to send him to college at the time his classmates went off to the University of Missouri. John could not afford to pay the university's tuition. Instead, Harry went to a commercial college for six months and continued taking piano lessons. In 1902 disaster struck as John's speculating in grain bankrupted the family. He lost $40,000—an immense sum of money, over a million dollars today—and the family lost the 160-acre farm that Martha had inherited from her father. John sold as many acres as he could, including the forty acres near Grandview that he had earlier bought. The family had to live in a rented house at 902 North Liberty Street until they moved, in 1903 to Kansas City, where John bought a modest house. The Truman curse of never being, or at least staying, wealthy struck for the first time, and haunted every year of Harry's life until he had the grand presidential salary. His father was a broken man. Harry stopped his piano lessons and dropped out of the commercial college. He took a job as a night watchman, the first time he was a salaried person. At eighteen, Harry was for a time the sole breadwinner of his family. He took a series of jobs—including one in the mailroom at the *Kansas City Star* for $7 a week, and another as a timekeeper for a railroad construction firm at $35 a month and board. A railroad foreman earthily remembered the young man as "all right from his asshole out in every direction." This crude characterization merely meant that Harry was an honest and hardworking clerk.

In 1903 Harry worked as a clerk at the National Bank of Commerce in Kansas City for $35 a month. He gained a reputation as an excellent worker. One supervisor wrote: "He was an exceptionally bright young man." His brother, Vivian, also worked at the bank but was rebellious, "without ambition," and ill-suited to indoor labor. Harry persevered on and off for two years and got a $5 raise. When his father moved the family to a new farm in March 1903, the boys quit to help, but were soon back at the bank. Before two months were up, Harry went to work at another bank, Union National Bank, at $60 a month. Soon, he was earning $100 a month. At $1,200 a year, he overmatched a teacher's salary of $358 a year. In today's money, an equivalent bank clerk would be making over $31,000.

While working at the banks, Harry lived in a boarding house in wide-open Kansas City. As though to keep temptation at bay, he gave himself only a dollar a week for recreation. At this time he chose to become a member of the Baptist Church. He preferred a direct line to the Lord over religions that mediated access through priests or clerics, prayer, and good works. A commentary on his banking career is that when he was at Commerce Bank another clerk was Arthur Eisenhower, brother of the future president. Arthur rose to be a senior executive in the early 1950s. That might be construed as the difference between a rock and a rolling stone. Also about this time, around 1906, Harry not only became a member of the National Guard but also tasted the cultural delights of the big city. He was at the two ends of the spectrum of activities. It was the beginning of a lifetime devotion to the military, with its male comradeship, so lacking in his adolescent years, discipline, and political relationships. Harry was a contented and rising, although minor, businessman, with male friends.

Kansas City had a large array of cultural amusements that interested Harry. He spent all of his spare money going out to worthy entertainments. We don't know what, if any, money he sent home, or what he might have saved. He went to the opera and to plays. The Metropolitan Opera—the finest in the country—came to town and performed *Parsifal, Lohengrin, Cavalleria Rusticana, Pagliacci,* and *Les Huguenots.* Harry went to concerts by pianists Josef Lhevinne and Ignacy Jan Paderewski. He loved plays, too, and vaudeville. George M. Cohan and Sarah Bernhardt were favorites. The plays he saw, either by buying a ticket or being an usher, included *Dr. Jekyll and Mr. Hyde* and Shakespeare's *Richard III, The Merchant of Venice, Julius Caesar,*

FIGURE 4 Harry Truman, at twenty-two, in his National Guard uniform, 1906. *Credit:* Cornish Paul Baker, courtesy of the Harry S. Truman Library.

and *Hamlet*. Harry lived a moral and chaste life at a time when single men, it was feared, alone in the city, would do otherwise. Kansas City was "a wild, concupiscent city," recalled the writer Edward Dahlberg. Harry avoided the wild and low life. He was exactly the kind of boy the rising Young Men's Christian Association provided room and board for. He did not need props like these to be good. His shyness with women led him to dreaming of a romantic relationship with Bess Wallace, who barely knew him. He saw her once in his adolescent years, but her crowd was not his.

At age twenty-two, Harry was content, single, and enjoying a rich cultural life of which his mother probably approved. Then his father ordered him to return home. For a second time, Harry's father pulled him from his heart's desire to be an independent and a successful businessman. The first time occurred when he did not go to college, as did his mother, and with his classmates. In March 1905, John had bought eighty acres to farm in Clinton with the money from his Kansas City house. Later that year, his corn crop was washed out. In October, the family went to live with Grandma Young, Harry's maternal grandmother, in Grandview, to work the farm. Harry appears to have been reluctant to give up his city life and job life, for it took months to get him back to the soil. He paid a high price as he was pulled toward his father, for he was a farmer from 1906 until he could escape to be a soldier in the greatest American adventure since the Civil War. How these farm years shaped Harry is conjectural. There was some joy that he was good at what he did, plowing very straight furrows, rotating crops every

FIGURE 5 Harry Truman riding a cultivator on the family farm in Grand-view, Missouri, ca. 1910. *Credit:* Harry S. Truman Library.

five years, and tending to farm animals. But the enormous isolation of hundreds of acres of empty space, quiet, and only one's thoughts to fill the day must have taken a toll on his psyche. He found time to read biography and some books recommended by Bess Wallace. He remembered: "I had memorized a whole book while plowing 40 acres." But he was lonely and out of place. He never wore the bib overalls that were usual for such work, and he sported a Panama hat, undoubtedly to keep him from getting sunburned and perpetually brown like his father. He looked different.

The Trumans were farming 600 acres, about four times the size of a normal Missouri farm. Grandmother Young owned most of it, but Harrison, who was losing interest in farming, had a good-sized piece. All got up at five in the morning and worked steadily for ten to twelve hours. But there were upsides. In his autobiography, Harry wrote, "Riding one of those plows all day, day after day, gives one time to think. I settled all the ills of mankind in one way or another while riding along seeing that each animal pulled his part of the load." He was a diligent, excellent worker, who put in twelve–sixteen-hour days. Such habits remained with him all the rest of his life, whether as a farmer, businessman, or politician.

Year after year—for ten years—Harry worked on the family farm, planting corn, sowing wheat and oats, running the binder to cut the wheat and oats, and pitching hay. He read various books and scientific works to create as modern a farm as possible, and the family vastly increased their crop yield. But the farm had good and bad years. Drought, animal diseases, John's broken leg, Harry's fractured leg, and other natural and human calamities marked Harry's agricultural life. In 1911 John made Harry a full partner and grandly made up stationery: "J.A. Truman and Son, Farmers." Records are scarce, and indicate that Harry wasn't much of a bookkeeper, even for the small income each year. Harry would now own land, but he was also now responsible for a half of John's debts.

It was said at the time by a neighbor that the Trumans were always broke. No one could figure out why, when others were prospering. When John died in 1914, he left Harry debts of $12,500—in today's money about $275,000. Two trials concerning the debt resulted in an out-of-court settlement. Harry

estimated that the one-half share of Grandma Young's lands was
worth $50,000. The settlement cost him $9,500 for quit claim
deeds. But Martha finally had her one-half share. Harrison
rented his share to Harry to farm. Martha quickly mortgaged
her land for $7,500, in part to pay lawyers' fees. The Trumans
finally had clear title to about 300 acres of prime lands by mid-
1914. They must have been land poor, however. Truman
recorded: "We always owed the bank something." He also recalled that the family "never made a dime" farming.

Harry had broken from the isolating, numbing, and back-
breaking farm work when he joined the Masons in 1909. For his
whole life, he was a staunch Mason, rising to its highest level.
(George Washington, James Monroe, Andrew Jackson, and both
Roosevelts were among the presidents who were also Masons.)
Like the Missouri National Guard, this was another all-male organization, whose comradeship he craved. His Masonic brothers
became as dear to him as his later army buddies. In addition,
Harry had already joined the Kansas City Athletic Club. At one
time or other, among many organizations, he became a member
of the Grandview Commercial Club, the town band, and the
Woodmen of the World. These were ways Harry coped with
being ordered back to farming, an occupation he never liked.

Another path leading out from farming was the business
world. Harry was attracted to many ventures, even though some
showed that he had little capacity to understand or manage
them. Getting money meant leaving the farm, and it brought
out a quiet rebelliousness or, perhaps on occasion, even, his father's recklessness in business. He looked for the main chance.

Harry put his back into ventures, yet he always thought that luck played a part in success. One had to seize the day. Then, it would always be easy to say, when one failed: "I was unlucky."

It is true that the Truman fortunes had taken a turn for the better when John became road overseer in 1912 for the southern half of Washington County. He saw that bridges and culverts were fixed, smoothed down the dirt roads, and collected the poll tax, which allowed one to vote. A man could pay the tax or work on the roads. Most farmers paid the money. The county court, an administrative body, appropriated the money; the overseer spent it and received county warrants for the bills rendered. These warrants could be cashed out for payment or made into promissory notes earning six percent. Banks discounted them and hoped for tax revenues to pay for them. John was fair toward his laborers. And he never cheated or kept the tax, as some overseers did. From his father's experience, Harry said: "I was taught that the expenditure of public money is a public trust and I have never changed my opinion on that subject." Harry, who of course later became a public servant, continued: "No one has ever received any public money for which I was responsible unless he gave honest service for it." Harry himself became road overseer in 1914. He also became postmaster at Grandview but gave the $50-a-month salary to the assistant postmistress to help her raise her family.

We have a very concise self-portrait of Harry in 1912: "a guy with spectacles and a girl mouth." He was unsuited to farming, not because he wasn't good at it—he was—but because he disliked the work, and his rising city career had been cut off by it.

As he looked at his life, he knew he had to reinvent himself, although no one used such a term at the time.

Harry's life from 1911 is recorded in a remarkable series of letters to Bess (she burned almost all of her replies to him). They are personal but mostly chart his many business ventures and heartbreaking failures. Bess Wallace lived nearby in an imposing, tall, gray house, with gingerbread fancies that Victorian architects loved. It was in the best neighborhood in town. The house had been built by her grandfather, George P. Gates, a wealthy man in the milling business. It was a showplace for formal dances, where women wore silk dresses and men sported tuxedos. Each day, dinner was served at two o'clock by servants—there was, also, always a cook, the latter someone the Trumans often had later in their lives, as Bess did not seem to be adept at the stove. A high tea must have sufficed in the evening. Harry was not an invited guest for some years after he met Bess. Then it was only on occasion. Bess did not consider Harry a suitable or important friend. The attraction was all on Harry's side.

For all of her life, Bess's mother never believed that Harry was worthy of Bess. Her daughter was a popular girl, tall, pretty, and well dressed. She was one of four children—she had three brothers—and an unusually skilled athlete. She played a wicked game of tennis, beating her brothers; skated in winter; and was a good dancer. Harry has never been known to dance, or to dance well, if he tried this activity. To no one of these sports and pleasures did Harry fit in, although, at one point, he tried to build a tennis court on the farm to lure Bess to visit and play, but she found it uneven and unplayable. Bess was popular with the boys, and several of them came from prosperous, elite families.

But a black cloud hung over her late adolescence and possible romances. In 1903 her father committed suicide at home. He was forty-three years old. Bess was eighteen and her brothers ranged from three to sixteen. David Wallace was alcoholic, and, as we know today, depression can either set off heavy drinking, or drinking can bring on depression. A serious illness, such as alcoholism or depression, often leads to suicidal thoughts and action. At the time these illnesses were thought moral lapses. Bess's immediate response to this tragedy was recorded by a friend: Bessie walked up and down outside her house with clenched fists, but was not crying. Her friend could say nothing to comfort a young girl whose life was shattered, except to join her in her walking.

The tragic suicide of David Wallace marked the life of her mother, Madge Gates Wallace, and the children of the family for their lifetimes, and it was a subject they almost never mentioned. Madge took her children to Colorado for a year to get away from the shame. Next to having a murderer in the family, or someone in prison, suicide was probably the worst thing that could befall a family in the Victorian social strata of the Gateses and Wallaces. For all her life, especially when Harry was a politician and president, Bess feared that this blemished past would be brought up to shame her. As a consequence, she lived as private a life as she could, and the suicide never became public knowledge. Truman protected this part of Bess's past with ferocity, even when their daughter, Margaret, wanted to know about family secrets.

Harry wrote to Bess with a confession before 1912: "All my girl friends [probably his cousins] think I am a cheerful idiot and a confirmed bachelor." In January 1912 he mentioned his goals in life: "I'd like to be rich for two reasons. First to pay my debts and give Mamma a fine house to live in, and, second and greatest I'd make love to you so hard you'd have to say yes or knock me on the head." He wasn't sure she cared for him even a little. Bess wrote to him: "A woman should think seriously only of a man who could support her in style." We know little more of Bess's views, as most of her letters were destroyed. But, she clearly shared her mother's view, that Harry was not good enough for her. She was higher in the social set and he was impecunious to boot.

Harry was undeterred by his own confessions and Bess's admonition. By 1912 he was in love. The letters continued. He seemed surprised that Bess went to the movies every night in the week. He did not surmise that Bess was escaping from life as the dutiful daughter to a now perpetually ailing mother. Two of her brothers would live in little cottages behind the Gates house, but they did not pitch in. We know from recently discovered letters by Margaret's son and published in 2011 that these two men were alcoholics who never amounted to much. This minor escape for Bess was an easy solution to the problem of her mother's utter dependence on her, which never sorted itself out in her lifetime.

Harry's letters to Bess, mostly signed "Yours sincerely," and occasionally and, boldly, "Your Harry," were often about his reading—they often traded titles—and his theatergoing. Books included Plato's *Republic,* the American Randall Parrish's novel *My Lady of Doubt,* and novels by the British writer Frances Hodgson Burnett. He was a serious reader, listing scores of titles over the years. And he was eager to show her that he read beyond magazines, especially his favorite, *Adventure.* How much of his daydreaming was to get away, one wonders. The many performances he went to included *Lucia di Lammermoor, Il Trovatore, Pinafore, The Man Without a Country,* and *The Prisoner of Zenda.* He often asked Bess to accompany him, but we do not always know when she did.

In June 1912, Harry asked Bess whether she would wear an engagement ring, if he bought "a solitaire." He called himself "a good-for-nothing American farmer." But, he added: "I've always had a sneakin' notion that someday maybe I'd amount to something." Bess said, "No." Harry hoped he could buy a car so that he could farm and court her at the same time. Sensing how things were going for Harry that fall, John Truman thought his romancing son was losing interest in farming, so he looked for a replacement laborer. Meanwhile, Harry continued to barrage Bess but knew he would have to become richer to be successful in his wooing.

By the end of 1913 Bess agreed to Harry's importuning. Now, however, it was Harry who was cautious. He asked for a secret engagement "to see how it feels." He mentioned that he was of "a timid disposition . . . and an enigma," the latter probably suggested by Bess in a missing letter, because he was willing to explain himself or remedy the situation. He still signed his letters, "Most sincerely." Bess's change of heart was also an enigma, unless she was in love with Harry. There is no evidence to point to any other conclusion.

But how could he afford to marry her? When John Truman died in 1914, his only bequest to Harry were the words "Never, never, give up" and the $12,500 debt. In 1916, Harry told Bess he did not have money to buy her an engagement ring after all. But when his uncle Harrison died later that year, leaving Harry $11,000, the young suitor immediately bought a fancy car for $650 so he could visit Bess more often. First things first.

Harry moaned to Bess in early 1916: "There is no one who wants to win half as badly as I do." That year, with some of the late Uncle Harrison's inheritance, he plunged into ventures in mining and oil to try to make his fortune. In the popular mind these failed entrepreneurial escapes are forgotten in favor of his unsuccessful haberdashery business. But they are significant for their intensity of effort, colossal mistakes, and broken dreams. With money from his mother, in exchange for some of Uncle Harrison's bequest to him, Harry became secretary-treasurer of a zinc and lead mine in Oklahoma. He was optimistic that he could make a go of it with his partners. "If the bloomin' thing fails to connect I'll be disappointed," he wrote to Bess. "You know I've got to win." He worked hard, even sleeping at the mine to save money. They struck lead and zinc, but a drunken superintendent cost them $1,000 by drilling wrong. He was optimistic, nevertheless. "I can't possibly lose forever," was his view. His triple life of running both the farm and the mine and courting Bess, however, proved impossible.

By May 1916 Harry was all confession and disappointment to her: "The mine has gone by the board. I have lost out on it entirely. . . . There was never one of our name who had sense enough to make money. I am no exception." He thought he could not soon recover financially, so he would return to the farm and wait for "something that will make money." He concluded with the surprising advice to Bess to find someone else. "My position seems to be that of following a mule up a corn row rather than directing the centers of finance."

The mine venture was not yet over, however. A banker friend, a fellow Mason, helped with cash. Harry still hoped to succeed and "to invest in some platinum ware" for Bess. He had to split his time, however, between running the mine—he was now its engineer—and saving the family farm. His sister, Mary Jane, was in charge of the farm, but the male farm workers would not work for a woman, so Harry went home to save the crops. Then it was back to the mine, which was, he reported to Bess, "in a dickens of a shape." He was in debt $5,500 and had to let some workers go.

Then, with no preparation, the optimistic Harry, not having had enough of a battering, allowed himself to be put forward in an election to be a Democratic Party committeeman. He lost this first venture into politics mostly because he was absent. Who knew him? As with his father, politics was a slight pulse. They had both attended a Democratic National Convention supporting William Jennings Bryan, but nothing else political can be found in their lives this early. Harry sometimes mentioned that politics might interest him, but it was as fleeting a thought as that of becoming rich. And then the mine venture failed, and he was out another $2,000. He wrote Bess: "There's nothing equals this business in making Micawbers of men." Like

Charles Dickens's character, Harry always felt that something was bound to turn up. Harry reckoned that he had had bad luck, and that others' "guesses" were just better than his. Indeed others struck rich veins of lead and zinc in locations where he had failed. Harry was now more heavily in debt. He thought of going into the auto business with a Ford dealership, which he calculated could earn him $5,000 a year. But he didn't.

Harry continued to daydream, in his Oz world: there, his debts would be paid and he would have a city home, a country house, some automobiles and flying machines and a yacht. We don't know how Bess took Harry's tongue-in-cheek possibilities. He thought he might have been better off staying on the farm, but he could not have meant this seriously. The mine finally closed in September 1916. But a banker friend still had confidence in him.

Irrepressible Harry was soon in the oil business out of Kansas City, with this friend. The company bought oil leases in Texas, Oklahoma, and Kansas. At first, only Harry put up cash. Then the partners established a brokerage firm in September 1916, with $5,000 Harry borrowed from his mother. He gave her, in return, a piece of property he had received on Uncle Harrison's death. He became treasurer of the company but did not draw his $250 monthly salary, as he was still running the farm. Harry reported to Bess in 1917: "The money is coming in by the basketful." At some point, she invested in the company. The major partner sold out, and a renamed company emerged. It put out glossy brochures and gave assurances about its prospects and value, as was usually done at the time. But the

venture was basically a wildcat operation, and few ever succeeded. The smartest investors usually got out early with profits, leaving others to mop up and in debt.

"If this venture blows, I'll know that I am hooded," Harry
wrote Bess. This was his state of mind in May 1917:

> I seem to have a grand and admirable ability for calling tails
> when heads come up. My luck should surely change. Some-
> time I should win. I have tried to stick. Worked, really did, like
> thunder for ten years to get that old farm in line for some big
> production. Have it in shape and have had a crop failure every
> year. Thought I'd change my luck, got a mine, and see what I
> did get. Tried again the other long chance, oil. Still have high
> hopes on that, but then I am naturally a hopeful, happy per-
> son, one of the "Books in brooks, Tongues in trees, and Good
> in everything" sort of guy.

Harry's only consolation was having Bess, "unless it is necessary for me to get myself shot in this war," he cryptically
added. At about this time Martha mortgaged her combined
farm for $25,000, about a fourth the value of the whole place.
There was probably a connection with Harry's new failure in
entrepreneurship.

Harry's ambition to be wealthy, to be free of family responsibilities, to be liked among male friends, had to be hidden, lest
he injure those dear to him by breaking away and breaking moral
commands to honor thy parents. The demands left a knot of
rage within him. How he coped with it, as his life unfolded, is

detailed later in his story. He had public and private bursts of temper and wrote harsh letters, which he usually never sent and were found in his desk after his death. Most of all, he suffered psychic pain, sending him into isolation; he holed up in hotels under assumed names, disabled. There he wrote memos or autobiographical fragments, many of which have survived. As early as 1911, Harry would mention stomach ailments when he was in acute distress.

On April 6, 1917, the United States declared war on Germany, and Harry enlisted in the army. He was thirty-two. His partners had let the company's lease in Eureka, Kansas "go to pot," as Harry noted, and another company struck oil at the fabulous Teter Pool, which made the owners very wealthy. Harry's company had leases near the Teter Pool; if they had only drilled more deeply, they would have struck oil. Harry's other ventures at the time were a land drawing in Dakota and a land lottery in Montana. The oil fiasco, however, rankled with Harry, for he figured: "If I'd stayed home and run my oil company I'd have been a millionaire." But then he added, "I would not have been president."

CHAPTER 2

CAPTAIN TRUMAN TAKES CHARGE

L eaving behind devastating losses in farming and business, Truman entered the army in April 1917, because, as he recorded: "I became all patriotic." Realistically, it was a good way to leave behind a life he did not care for, except for having Bess in it. He told her that they ought not to get married, as she now wanted, because he might not come back at all, or he might return injured. Bess's romantic turnaround remains a mystery, as she left no letters behind. We must simply assume she was in love and, perhaps, wanted a child. But she took Harry's decision well, they continued to write to each other, and he called whenever he could commandeer a phone. And she sent him a lovely picture of herself that he carried with him for the whole time he was in the war.

What had been happening from 1914 to 1917? On a sunny day, cloudless and bracing, the guns of August boomed out, beginning the most devastating war in Europe since Napoleon's

FIGURE 6 Portrait of Bess Wallace, ca. 1917, which Harry carried with him to France during World War I. *Credit:* Harry S. Truman Library.

reign. Leaders stumbled into war because they were overwhelmed by events and proceeded heedlessly toward a catastrophe. A Serbian had killed the Archduke of Austria, Russia allied with the Serbs, and Germany took Austria's side. It was an incident that touched off a firestorm that had been simmering for years. The war was fought across the huge land mass of Europe, utterly destroying towns and countryside and decimating armies. The naval war was equally destructive. By 1917 British casualties were a quarter million men. By war's end Germany and France had lost two million men. Epic battles caught the imagination of those following the war, but not Harry, with the sides seesawing on an almost static front. Nineteen seventeen culminated in the "breaking of the armies." Battles such as Arras, Ypres, Verdun, the Marne, and the Somme were etched as great slaughterhouses. Early casualties in the Battle of the Somme in July 1916, for example, were 160,000 for the Germans and 200,000 for the French and British. Barely three miles changed hands. At battle's end the Germans and the Allied forces each lost 600,000 men. It was a tragedy of immense proportions in all of military history, and for families and national psyches. The memory of World War I is truly that of the Somme, the loss of a generation of young men for a cause that seemed nebulous to the common soldier.

In his numerous letters to Bess before 1917, Harry appears oblivious to European events, as he tells her of business deals and his dreams of wealth, and wanting to marry her if only he had the wherewithal. Bess was supportive of Harry's fruitless endeavors, for he told her he saw "rainbows in the darkest sky." It was clear that she would never marry a man with no prospects, or one who had not already arrived. He was grateful that she was "not very angry" with him as he was irretrievably failing in business by mid-July of 1916. "Reverses make a man or a mouse," he wrote Bess. He was hanging on by his "eyebrows." He needed "consolation" from her. While war raged in Europe, he playfully suggested names for Bess's new dog: Don Juan of Austria, Caesar, Kitchen, after Lord Kitchener, Willy, for William Jennings Bryan, Villa, for Pancho Villa. In a serious vein, Harry wrote Bess on May 27 that if he could not win "straight," that is, honestly, he would continue to "lose." Heaven knows what shenanigans he chose to avoid, or was he making an excuse for failure? To balance the "direful" financial difficulties, he would have her. It would be a heavenly situation. He wrote to Bess on July 14, 1917, that he felt like a "dog," because he had joined the army and the decision had made her "unhappy." It had also brought "two big tears" to his mother's eyes.

"Maybe a little war experience will tone me down and make a man of me. I hope it will anyway," he insightfully wrote. "All I ask is love me always."

Truman had been a member of the Missouri National Guard until 1911, and when in 1917 President Woodrow Wilson called up those troops, he signed up again. He could have stayed home, given his poor eyesight. But he obviously wanted to go, and so he memorized the eye chart for his physical. At any rate, with his eyeglasses he had perfect vision. But his poor eyesight was not the only reason he could have been exempted from wartime military service. There were two others: not only was he the mainstay of his family, he was also a farmer. (Once he enlisted, he turned over the farm to his mother and sister, who ran it with hired labor.) There was even a fourth out: at thirty-two, he was beyond draft age. But he wanted to go. Soon, the Guard was merged with the army, and Truman was off to the war, with training, poor at best in the Guard, as an artilleryman.

There was hostility between the National Guard troops and the regular army throughout the war, so Truman had to work hard to prove himself. Diligence, good work habits, and character stood him in very good stead. His intelligence and learning from his vast reading of history were other supports. In France during the war, soldiers were always amazed by how much he knew about earlier, historic battles in Europe. And he had another great advantage: the ability to be affable, to get along with other men, honed from all the voluntary groups he had joined, especially the Masons. He knew when to win over other men with praise and encouragement, as well as to be stern when it came to questions of principle.

Truman quickly became known in his battery as a good clerk, efficient and friendly. He was just five feet eight, a bit round, bespectacled, and neat as a pin. He took pride in his new status. He kept up writing in a number of notebooks about his military life and battles and wrote incessantly to Bess about what was going on. Hundreds of letters survive that are a treasure trove for historians. Truman later wrote memoirs, autobiographies and notes, mostly accurate on events, that allow us to relive his interior and exterior life.

Truman was among only a handful of men preceding him as president who saw active combat—the most famous being George Washington, Andrew Jackson, Ulysses S. Grant, William McKinley, and Theodore Roosevelt. Except for the irrepressible Roosevelt, none left us with firsthand accounts of wartime life. Certainly, the war experience helped shape all these warrior presidents. Truman's war was the petri dish for his later political leadership. And while the war would destroy a generation of European men, it would make a man of Truman.

Harry had been a corporal in Battery B when he was in the Missouri National Guard. When the Guard was judged of insufficient size for war, it grew into Batteries B and C and became a regiment. In June 1917, Truman was assigned to Battery F of the Second Missouri Field Artillery and was chosen to be first lieutenant. This honor was a great surprise to him, as his level of manly self-confidence was not terribly high. Missouri and Kansas units then formed the new Thirty-fifth Division. Battery F had a full complement of 145 men by July. In August, the Missouri National Guard was called into federal service as the 129th Field Artillery. The army organized three field artillery units at this time, and the 129th was one of them. The command was the Sixtieth Field Artillery Brigade.

In August 1917, Truman was off for a seven-month tour to Camp Doniphon at Fort Sill, Oklahoma, known for its dust and mosquitoes as much as for its training. Truman described his new post to Bess: "Batteries and flying machines, balloons and doughboys are as thick as girls on Petticoat Lane." When Truman could find no army equipment to unload the gear, he offered his hot, bright red, Stafford Touring car. He also brought his own horse, a fine, sturdy, farm-bred animal, even though he would be supplied two horses by the army. He was a superb horseman, a talent that would be of tremendous help in the war.

Truman's claim to fame in this dreary outpost was his running of the best and most profitable canteen on the base, an achievement that earned him the dubious nickname of "Truman *heinies.*" From this success, Harry would take away the wrong lesson, when after the war he plunged into the haberdashery

FIGURE 7 "A jolly bunch," at the 129th Field Artillery Canteen, Camp Doniphan, Oklahoma, 1917. Harry Truman is the fifth from the right. The soldiers are drinking refreshments from Truman's canteen. Eddie Jacobson is among the men standing, seventh from left. *Credit:* F. G. Willard, courtesy of the Harry S. Truman Library.

business, in a competitive, uncertain marketplace unlike the closed economic system of the army base.

The army was giving Truman an education befitting an officer of artillery who had not gone to college. In a standard sixteen-week program, he was taught college-level mathematics, logarithms, square roots, trigonometry, navigation, and logistics. He didn't think he was being trained to hit targets directly, the army not bothering to explain that indirect firing was being taught. This new tactic, indirect firing, is used when gunners do not have a direct line of sight on a target, so they must calculate artillery fire based on azimuth and elevation angles. It is a fine art. In addition, using indirect firing, the artillery would soften up and injure the enemy as much as possible before an advance. This was a newer French tactic that Truman would also study at training school in France. Meanwhile, the men trained with three-inch cannons. Not until June 1918 would they get twenty-four French 75mm rapid-fire guns, the finest

of Allied artillery. Now, the units were short of ammunition, guns, and even soldiers, yet the men struggled to learn. Battery F was gaining a reputation as the best unit.

December 1917 was a month of great events, personal and military, for Harry Truman. He was given two weeks' leave to go home and to see Bess. They knew it would be the last they would see each other until he returned from the war, if he returned. Militarily important was the news that his battery would soon be issued those fine French 75mm guns. For the moment they were given the instruction manual for the guns, but Harry and some others were chosen to leave Camp Doniphon to attend special artillery officers' training in France, as part of the Thirty-fifth Division. It was an honor for a non-college man to be selected. At about this time, also, two men came into his life who would be essential parts of his later political career: Lieutenants Harry Vaughan and Jim Pendergast. After the war, Pendergast, from Kansas City, introduced Truman to his powerful political family, which became the linchpin of Truman's political career. And Harry Vaughan would decades later become military aide to President Truman and serve through the entire presidency of his old friend.

Truman and his unit were among seven thousand men who sailed to France on the *USS George Washington*. After thirteen days at sea, they landed on April 13, 1918, on one of the few sunny mornings of Harry's time in France. Usually, for months on end, bad weather would be the soldiers' curse. The war was being fought on both sides from trenches, and the constant rain made mud bogs, sometimes as deep as six feet, of all of the

Western Front. In such conditions, cannon and horses moved slowly or not at all. And by 1918, the French horses were of poor quality and weakened by war, the best having already been exhausted and killed. Roads, if they existed at all, were barely passable. Thrust into this environmental disaster, Truman's men became acclimated, sourly, and he went to training school to learn how to fire the French 75mm gun.

Much happened in the next three months that would shape Truman's character for the rest of his days. On April 27, Truman and Battery D went to Brittany in northwestern France, for a brief stay at the Coëtquidan training school, which had been founded by Napoleon. Then they moved to eastern France, to Montigny-sur-Aube and the Second Corps Field Artillery School, a modern, no-nonsense artillery training school, which gave a six-week intensive course of study. Truman studied surveying, geometry, and astronomy there to learn his new trade. On May 19, 1918, he wrote Bess, "We have been working harder than ever. I had an examination Saturday that would make the president of Yale University bald-headed scratching his head trying to think for answers. I think we'll be nuttier than an Arkansas squirrel if we study this harder any longer."

After finishing the training course, Truman taught what he had learned to the college-educated officers. He wrote to Bess, "You should see me hand these fellows bunk and make them like it. It's rather funny for an old rube to be handing knowledge (of a sort) to the Harvard and Yale boys. . . . The hardest work I ever did in my life, too. I'd rather saw wood or pitch hay." He never got over not going to college, envied those who had gone, and preferred the company of his noncommissioned acquaintances to that of his fellow officers. Looking back on July 22, 1918, when he now had his own battery to command, he confessed to Bess, "I never knew how valuable a university education is until now."

On June 14, Harry wrote Bess that he had "just barely slipped through the artillery school." The best students would stay on as instructors and never see action. He calmly wrote, "I am glad I didn't make any such record." He was now adjutant of the second Battalion, 129th Field Artillery Regiment, "a right hefty job and one that gives me precedence over all the Battery Captains, even if they do outrank me. I've got to organize a regimental school and teach the balance of the officers what I learned (which won't be a whole lot)." He was outside the formal chain of command but openly wanted his own battery.

On July 11, 1918, Truman, now a captain, was given command of Battery D, of the 129th Field Artillery Regiment. It was a wild and insubordinate unit. Truman was their fourth commander. He wrote that when he took over, "Much of the battery—including six sergeants—was under arrest, in quarters." The charges included "drunkenness, refusal to obey orders and failure to report for reveille." What the miscreants saw before them was "a rather short fellow, compact, serious face, wearing glasses." Truman said nothing, and dismissed them. He then called a meeting of his noncommissioned officers to read them the riot act: "I am sure you men know the rules and regulations. *I* will issue orders and *you* are responsible for them being carried out. . . . I didn't come over here to get along with you.

You've got to get along with me. If there are any of you who can't, speak right now, and I'll bust you right now." The boys tested Truman twice by letting horses loose to run riot and by getting drunk and playing craps. Truman retaliated by demoting more than half his non-coms. Then he promoted four of his men to sergeant. As one soldier observed, "This cookie means business." Truman kept up the discipline with punishments and rewards, even trying to get one soldier court-martialed. When he failed in this punishment, he transferred out many trouble-makers. Within ten days, Battery D was subdued. As one soldier later put it: "He not only commanded the outfit, he owned it."

By leading Battery D, Truman had achieved, he wrote Bess on July 14, his "one ambition. . . . If I can only make good at it, I can hold my head up anyway the rest of my days." Two weeks later, Harry wrote Bess that his battery was the best in the school. But then there was a very human confession: "I have my doubts about bravery when heavy-explosive shells and gas attacks begin. . . . I have the bravest kind of head and body but my legs won't stand."

Truman was among the first American soldiers to go into battle in the Great War. His regiment was a part of a military section that had barely moved in four years of war in the Vosges Mountains in eastern France near the German border. Moving out across France from "fairy-tale" Paris, going southeast, Battery D was one of eight, separated by an hour's train distance for safety. The trains did not stop at all in the three-day journey. Battery D's trains included almost fifty cars carrying guns, caissons, kitchens, extra rations, horses, hay and feed, fire control

FIGURE 8 Captain Harry S.
Truman, Battery D, 129th
Field Artillery, expert horse-
man, July 1918. *Credit:* Arthur
W. Wilson, courtesy of the
Harry S. Truman Library.

instruments, mechanics' tools, a first-class coach for Truman
and his lieutenants, and much else.

In the middle of the night on August 20, 1918, the train
stopped at Saulxures, which was, as one officer recalled, "a beautiful French village." An off-loading lieutenant was charmed by
the scene as morning broke and left a recollection of this as yet
unscarred dreamscape:

It nestled among the mountains, or the beginnings of the
mountains, on the banks of the Moselotte, and was clean, prosperous and attractive. Near the eastern end of the long main
street was a large public fountain, with a big trough, rectangular

and divided into compartments, in which, respectively, horses were watered, laundry done, and water drawn. Farther down was the substantial, spired church, with its adjoining cemetery, and across from it the Mairie or City Hall, where our regiment had its headquarters. Pretty good stores, not large, but with a fair supply of necessities and reasonable luxuries, were to be found; and a hotel where a most creditable and appetizing meal could be had.

Truman's Battery D was assigned to the front on August 21 and took positions in foothills high in a site 2,200 feet above the valley floor at the commune of Kruth. When set up, his guns were higher up, at 3,870 feet. The climb up for Battery D was excruciatingly hard, even with the help of an old cable car. The section Truman's men were entering had been quiet, and a status quo obtained. The Germans fired lackadaisically, and even put up in a front-line trench a large banner reading: "Welcome 35th Division." Astoundingly, the French and Germans had been sharing a lake to bathe in on alternate days. All that foolery ended when the Americans arrived.

The three batteries of Captain Truman's Second Battalion were spread over seven kilometers. Battery D was part of a cluster intended to rain down fire on Germans. Truman was in a hurry to get his men and guns in position. The Germans went on the alert. But suddenly he was diverted from this necessary work and invited to dine with the American and French commanders. The toasts to President Wilson, Marshal Ferdinand Foch, King George, and General Pershing were all well and good but seemed unnecessary to him in war, and he felt that having each course set with different clean plates wasted precious time. Still, they had time to view the battle map. The French had exquisitely produced terrain maps. After all, they had been preparing for war with Germany since they had lost the strategic and rich Alsace-Lorraine on their border to it in the war in 1870, when Emperor Napoleon III thought he could best Germany. Now, Truman received orders for an entirely new position for his guns, no longer trained on Kruth. They were to be placed, he wrote, "just in under the edge of the forest, with an open meadow lying before us and the enemy's position across a valley." The meadow was two kilometers long. The men worked to the point of exhaustion to get into place, stopping only for a supper of cold beans, corned beef, and PET evaporated milk. They picked wild red raspberries. A Frenchman had brought along a bottle of champagne. This French-American potluck must have seemed fortifying ambrosia to these weary soldiers as they prepared for the great battle ahead.

Truman and his men went up "a tortuous wooded track" to get ready. They camouflaged their site, emplaced the guns, and set up camp. Some of the men misbehaved, once more, but Truman had received his orders and the men, with the help of too few tired draught horses, worked their way up the mountain. Clink, clash, bump, snort, went men and animals all night. It was a smooth operation. The men built Truman's command post and defensive bunkers. They temporarily ran out of food, and communication was sporadic. Clouds, rain, and haze would make firing haphazard. Truman worked out his coordinates but never fired a shot. Then his battery was ordered to prepare a poison gas bombardment in the high Vosges for four the next morning, probably August 22. This would be their first engagement. Truman was overcome with a "real creepy feeling," he later recalled, but, as he said, he "never felt about . . . later encounters exactly as I did that first one." Suddenly the Germans fired gas shells at Battery D. Truman withdrew from his position. It was a good move, because none of his soldiers got wounded or killed, although there were casualties among the horses. Two of Battery D's men were later cited for courage. Not all had gone well, however. Truman had given duties to an old soldier, a veteran of the Mexican campaign of 1916, out of respect for his age, but he was not up to his job. And the old soldier's negligence almost got the battery slaughtered.

On August 29, the battery fired hundreds of gas rounds at the enemy. They were mostly shells filled with a newer gas, phosgene. (Three poison gases were used by both sides in the war: chlorine, phosgene, and mustard. Phosgene is a choking pulmonary poison that stays close to the ground.) At eight that evening Truman's gunners fired in five three-minute bursts of one hundred rounds, then rounds against a second and third and fourth target followed in an irregular pattern. All this took thirty-six minutes. Truman's men hoped that the irregular nature of the attack would catch Germans off guard, without their new improved gas masks, and would inhibit a quick counterattack. Then Truman's battery got off another 490 rounds in fifteen minutes. One gun fell behind schedule. Truman waited for the missing gun, bogged down in the mud, to show up, even

though his men were now open to German fire. He was not
going to break off, even temporarily. Two gunners started to
pull back, away from German fire, and two more were readied
in place. Then Harry's horse threw him, but he remounted and
resumed command. He ordered that nine horses be used to pull
out the gun mired in the mud. When the Germans returned
fire, some of his men started to run away, but Truman cursed at
them to come back. Battery D reorganized and got out of danger, and no German gas shells reached them.

The battery moved away from German range, and Truman
felt ashamed that he had to leave two guns behind in the mud.
But his gas attack had achieved its main goal; it had stopped
German retaliation. The Germans did fire back, but a benefit
of the pervasive deep mud was that it simply absorbed German
shells, almost swallowing them up. Harry wrote Bess that one
shell exploded fifteen feet away from him "and I didn't get a
scratch." The mud, which had dogged the American army all
summer, had turned into a friend. Their battle over, Truman
and his men had some time to restore their energy. They got
hot food, and Captain Truman slept for twelve whole hours.
One gunman was demoted to private for errors, and another
was promoted. Then they retrieved their mud-encased guns.

Later, the whole episode—the men's first taste of war, some
of the men starting to run away, Truman cursing them to get
back—was jokingly dubbed "The Battle of Who Ran." Of Truman, one corporal wrote, "We have a captain who cannot be
beaten." Less heroic, Truman reported to Bess: "My greatest
satisfaction is that my legs didn't succeed in carrying me away,

although they were anxious to do so." Then he grew poetic after his encounter with death and about her role in his life. Loosely quoting his "pet poet" Lord Byron on the Assyrians in "The Destruction of Sennacherib," he wrote that her letters were "like stars seen in the blue waves that roll nightly on deep Galilee."

The actions of Battery D were part of the greater war, of course, and of the first, large American offensive. The attack involved using nine divisions against the Germans' puncture into the Allied line at the commune of Saint-Mihiel in the Meuse department in northeast France. So, Truman's unit was ordered out of its entrenched position and off on a 125-mile movement to be made mostly at night. He wrote up his exploits of Saint-Mihiel in his military *Notes,* preserved in the Truman Library in Independence, Missouri, and in a long letter to Bess, starting on September 2, all of which are the stuff of the following account, along with other soldiers' reminiscences. Very pertinent to these events were three weeks of driving rain.

One soldier, Lieutenant Jay Lee, left a poetic account of those first three weeks of September:

> We sometimes went so far as 30 or 35 kilometers in a night; which wasn't so bad except when, as so often happened, obstructions or congestions in the road caused those long and tiresome, or frequent, fretful, stops and starts. The wondrous fact of all these men over there made a vivid and solemn impression, whether marching in the moonlight, with long lines of horses, limbers, guns, caissons and men stringing out interminably before and behind; or in the dark, cloudy, rainy

nights, with only vague shadows immediately in front, and vague noises beyond; and in either case the silent, monotonous, steady forward movement of thousands of men, all alike in outward appearance of round-topped helmet and army raincoat; all with a common purpose and determination, but each occupied with his own thoughts; silent, spectral, inevitable. Once in a while one will address you; and the contrast, the sharpness of the break, almost startles you.

The only benefit from the rain and mud was that the German artillery was silent during the battery's march.

The Battle of Saint-Mihiel raged from September 11 to the 16th. It was the first great American offensive. But Truman wrote that for the three first days he did not get a chance to fire a shot. Sometime after that, however, "I fired 3000 rounds of 75mm ammunition from 4:00 AM to 8:00 AM around the town of Boureuilles." Boureuilles was in the sector that was the responsibility of the Twentieth Division Regiment, not Truman's Thirty-fifth. There were strict rules about staying in sector. Firing out of sector could result in court-martial. But Truman's battery blew up three German batteries, and, as he later recalled, "I saved some men of the twentieth division on our left and they were grateful." There was nothing of the martinet about Captain Truman. He took initiatives in the war to protect his fellow soldiers and pound the Germans.

The Meuse-Argonne offensive, a decisive engagement, began on September 26 and lasted to the end of the war on November 11, 1918. French and American forces totaled 550,000, while the Germans had only 190,000. The Thirty-fifth Division would be one of the units to lead the way. In his *Notes* Truman recounted that Battery D had had ten days to get to the line, as hundreds of thousands of troops headed to the new battlefield. The roads were more than overcrowded. Truman and his men endured nights of forced marches in the pelting rain. The men were "almost dead on [their] feet," and horses dropped dead. Truman's colonel, whom many considered crazy, ordered him to double-time the men. Truman pretended to misunderstand the order and told them to rest. His men thought he would be court-martialed, but he wasn't. Truman also talked this same colonel out of court-martialing men for not keeping up with the battery. The colonel gave Truman a tongue-lashing. Truman wrote, "The Colonel insults me shamefully. No gentleman would say what he said. Damn him." The colonel committed suicide in 1925 with his army gun.

The Meuse-Argonne campaign, the great offensive that won the war, was the pinnacle of Truman's army career. He left drafts of these events at the time and later, as well as a typed version, and recounted the fight in a key letter to Bess. With other sources, it is possible to re-create his fighting role. Truman's gunners struggled to get into position on September 22–23. It had been "the wildest ride" he had experienced in the year, he commented. The 129th Field Artillery's position was between the Argonne Forest and Verdun. Truman wrote, "It was a heart-breaking job. The fields were muddy and full of shell holes. Carriages would get stuck and horses fall down; men would slip into shell holes half filled with water. . . . They got into position by 3 AM and under cover." As another historian of Truman's war years wrote, "Truman's unit was at the end of the westward-pointing V's southern arm, and thus was the farthest to the rear of the artillery battery—French or American—in the brigade sector." On the 24th, German shelling missed his unit, but the next day, a shell knocked out their kitchen. The Germans had not thought that the Allies would enter another big battle so soon after St. Mihiel, but the Americans were positioning themselves near the French sector between the Argonne Forest and Verdun. The Germans had guessed wrong.

September 26 was the D-day for the Allies to move against the Germans in a massive offensive. Truman briefed his sergeants about the timing, range, and elevation of the guns and the importance of the coming battle. The outcome would determine who would be the victor and who the vanquished in the epic struggle. When the artillery barrage was under way, he recalled, "I was as deaf as a post. It looked as though every gun in France was turned loose and the sky was red from one end to the other from the artillery flares." The 129th fired 13,000 rounds. Battery D fired 2,018 rounds. The barrage was staged ahead of the infantry—the new tactic of the war. Truman's guns got so hot, they fell behind the pace in order to cool down.

When the battery guns were cooling, the tanks took up the slack. Colonel George S. Patton Jr., head of the new Tank Corps, won his spurs in the Argonne, with his fast-moving juggernauts. But the squishy ground, or "General Mud" as some called it, slowed down the new gun emplacement, and for a time Truman had only one gun in use. He was supposed to find Patton and liaise with him to cover the latter's armor. But so swift were Patton's movements, Truman could find neither a tank nor an infantry commander to support. The American army had penetrated three and a half to four miles into the salient, although in an uneven way, with two miles lost on the right flank, which was caught in the dense foliage of the Argonne Forest. Battery D's guns were ordered into no-man's-land. The battery formed at the rear of the regiment but soon caught up and reached the safety of the more open, but still protective, woods.

About some of his upcoming movements, Truman was not too accurate in his recountings, but the indefatigable Truman's men crossed the muddy bog to get into position. He later recalled, "It was the worst night I ever spent. Men went to sleep standing up and I had to make them keep on working." Now the command structure gave confusing orders. Captain Truman had to use his good sense to react. He considered the first order, an attack order, "nonsensible," an "impossible to-carry-out fire mission." Then there was a new order: to fire at 5 AM, the next day, September 27, but he did not, because the order got to him an hour late, and there was no time to prepare the guns by raising them high enough to shoot over and protect the advancing infantry. As a result, not a shot was fired by Truman and two nearby batteries, for fear of hitting the troops. Other batteries, elsewhere, were able to fire. "This was the only time in the whole drive that the regiment did not fire every time it was called on to do so," Truman commented in one of his several accounts of this day, a long hand-written draft in his *Notes*.

Truman and Battery D moved to a place along the German Scorpion trench system, which was rightly called a "cemetery of the unburied dead." Battery D was directed to the left flank.

There they found they had to chop down trees to get a line of fire, and thus Truman's guns started firing an hour late. It was a delay he was sensitive about, but there was nothing he could do. That day, his men were bombed by a German plane, but the attack killed only some horses.

After the battle, Truman was sent out on reconnaissance in Charpentry and suddenly found that he was accidentally beyond the front line, which had just been pulled back. He hurried back. Again, planning for a new attack was delayed because of clogged roads. Truman was supposed to support Patton, but for three days he could do little. The mission of the Thirty-fifth and Twenty-eighth Divisions was to plunge ahead into the Argonne Forest. The expectation was that the Germans would withdraw, but they didn't. Truman's observation post allowed him to spot nearby Germans, but they were outside his area, and orders were to stay in one's designated sector. Nevertheless, because Truman surmised that the German gunners would soon be firing on the Thirty-fifth, he got permission to fire and took out the German battery using only forty-nine rounds (it usually took 500 rounds to knock out a battery). Truman was satisfied, but his nemesis colonel again wanted him court-martialed for firing out of sector.

The battle was beyond fierce, with casualties heavy and the men in hell. A German airplane spotted Truman's men, but they moved just in time from their site, which soon came under heavy bombardment. The number of wounded mounted, and clogged roads made getting aid to them difficult. For thirty hours, 2,400 men lay in the mud, sleet and rain pelting them.

Some had lost limbs, all were in some kind of pain. Battery D watched in horror. They did not have any litters to carry the wounded or blankets to keep them warm. Truman and his commander observed the situation. But the commander did not do what seemed obvious to the sensible Truman. He did not order that the artillery guns be rotated to target the German observation positions, which were out of sector. On his own, Truman ordered Battery D's guns to rotate and fire sixty-four rounds in a few minutes, despite the recent memory of his risking a court-martial for a similar order. Then Battery D fired on a moving German battery, and the Germans deserted their guns. Truman wasn't sure how well his guns had done and admitted to his colonel that he had flagrantly disregarded his commander's orders. The colonel responded: "You got them all right." They found six abandoned German guns. This event took place at the edge of the woods of the Argonne Forest, full of German machine-gun nests.

Truman's unit now joined other batteries, firing a "furious" 715-round barrage. General Pershing wanted a war of movement. He was setting up a pincer attack and needed speed and judgment by officers. Then on September 28, the army suffered great losses because of the very rule that Truman had broken several times to positive effect. Pershing was aghast when he learned about gunners not being allowed to fire out of sector. "But surely you do not obey that order?" he asked an officer in the field. Pershing's personal visit to the field allowed him to find out what was going on. He learned that American guns had been firing on targets far in the German rear and not on the forest because the Thirty-fifth had not asked for assistance. The chain of command that had once threatened Truman for firing out of sector—that is, for using his initiative—was now using his initiative to ward off criticism of themselves. These regular army officers, when blame was cast for immense losses and bumbling, threw it onto the National Guard, indicating they were inferior soldiers. Truman called these men The West Point Protective Association. Truman felt ill-used. His men were in action against nearby machine-gun nests, but not where the division's infantry was. Battery D, while certainly arrayed for action, never fired a shot to cover the infantry. But, after the war, a soldier recollected that Battery D wiped out machine-gun nests and anti-tank guns. Army disarray and blaming the National Guard lingered with Truman for over thirty years, even to his considering closing West Point when he was president. And as senator he asked to be put on a military affairs committee.

For two days, September 28 and part of the 29th, the front was quiet. Truman's unit was far behind the infantry. In fact, none of the 75mm batteries could give fire support because the terrain made it difficult to move the battery's heavy guns. So they were ordered to give useless, harassing fire. Truman thought this order of fire "questionable." There was no tight choreography of various troops. In fact, the infantry didn't receive any morale-boosting benefit since the battery's shots could be neither seen nor heard.

American mistakes abounded as German units started moving again on the 29th. The flat terrain and the 75mm guns kept Battery D from action, as they fired only directly and the American infantry was moving down a steep slope. What was needed were howitzers, since they could travel high and plummet at a steep angle, but these gunners had none. Battery D was moved around and was ordered to fire 641 rounds as the American army retreated under shelling by gas and explosives, but it managed only 101 undirected rounds. There were severe infantry losses. German artillery was working effectively, and Allied artillery was not. At this point, Truman was ordered to protect his big guns with his anti-aircraft guns.

On this fateful day, September 29, Truman's position was not bombarded. He was ordered, or took the initiative, to fire his guns furiously, 117 rounds in ten minutes. But the large battle was lost, as Germans threw back assaults of the two American divisions. American losses were grievous. Battery D was on the same ground on day four of the battle, September 30, as on day two. Truman's men were told to remain in place to cover relief efforts and support the infantry, until the division's own guns could be brought in. Then the battery's guns were suddenly peppering the Germans. It is not known who ordered this barrage, but it saved American lives. Some soldiers credited Truman with their survival, while others praised the major in charge. Whatever the case, Truman's men continued to fire, but now more leisurely because the Germans chose not to attack. That day one of Truman's guns misfired, the only time that happened in the whole campaign. September 30 to October 1 was quiet, and the men slept.

On October 2, Truman's men engaged in fast barrages. They were not returned. October saw a massive barrage of persistent gas aimed at the Germans. Truman made up his firing plan to draw Germans out as they tried to escape the gas attack. Then the order came for the infantry to postpone its activity. Battery D harnessed and hitched up and moved off away from the battlefield. The men were due a week's rest at Signeulles, near Saint-Mihiel, starting on October 5.

Since July 17 Battery D had fired 8,385 rounds and had traveled more than 200 miles over hellish terrain to join the fight. Their guns were so well maintained that superiors considered them the best of all the artillery. But the efforts of Truman and his men had their price, and the men were showing the effects of the war. Truman had lost twenty-five pounds, and his men were "scarecrows," he later wrote. But when he told Bess about events, he said that he was "fat, healthy, and bulletproof." He was always tender toward her and protected her from the horrors of the war.

The Thirty-fifth Division had experienced enormous losses of foot soldiers in the campaign. There were about 50 to 80 percent casualties among the front-line units. In four days of fighting in the Meuse-Argonne, the division suffered 8,023 casualties out of almost 27,000 men—the highest daily loss rate of any American division during the war. Artillery casualty rates, however, were light in comparison. One hundred forty-six artillerymen of the Thirty-fifth Division died. Battery D was the lucky unit, with no losses, and it and its captain were on top of the world. "We'll go in again, when our time comes," Truman wrote to Bess. Always trying to be upbeat, Truman continued to protect her from the ghastly events in the war. "The Prussian Guards simply can't make their legs stand when they get word that the Yanks are coming." But the war droned on.

From October 12 to 16, the Thirty-fifth Division and Sixtieth Field Artillery were headed to the front to drive into Germany, first crossing the Meuse River. They moved toward the main German rail link. They passed old French forts that had been the scene of epic struggles two years before at Verdun, when 434,000 Germans and 542,000 Frenchmen were casualties, half of them dying. One officer, Lieutenant Jay Lee, could not resist painting in words what the Americans beheld. It is vivid and better than any historian's treatment:

> The Meuse River, like the Missouri, meanders lazily hither and yon in a broad valley, frequently overflowing its banks, and never of certain channel. For water traffic, a well dredged canal has been constructed along the east edge of the bottom-land. In places the range of hills known as the Meuse Heights comes so close to the canal that there is just room between the two for the National Highway which during the war constituted one of the main traffic roads from the direct south and from the rail-head at Rattentout, to the chain of forts which constituted the permanent forts of Verdun on the east, and to the front lines which were strung out in the valley below the eastern slope of the hills. The road and canal though not visible from the enemy's lines, except possibly at certain points from balloons, were yet more or less constantly

under fire; for the Germans of course realized their importance as an avenue for supplies, and it was easy to lay on them with their long range guns.

Riding along this road toward the front, after a week's freedom from any fear of hostile shells, our men could hear, but paid little attention to, the never-ceasing but gradually more distinct roar of distant artillery. As they rode, away off to the right, five or six miles away, the muffled "boom" of some German large calibers sounded. A few moments of indifference as before—then—a sudden thrill of realization as out of the atmosphere comes that wicked "Br-r-r-r-r," and—"Bang!" a shell bursts on the hillside above them. Another moment of silence, then from one of them: "Gee! I swallowed my chew!"

Truman's battery shared the scene and the screeching German shells.

On October 18, Truman's men fired barrages to protect the infantry and stuck their necks out more than other gunners to do so, for any firings would be detected by the Germans, who would reply with accuracy. Truman thought that having all units fire at once was dangerous because guns overheated and would have to cool down, all at the same time, leaving the infantry unprotected. Some of his superior officers at first questioned Truman's idea, considering him "impertinent," but the command quickly changed their orders, and Truman's plan to fire barrages in relays was deemed "arguably more effective at protecting the infantry."

From October 18 to 29, Battery D was quiet. Truman thought this ending of the firing was the result of the army's incompetence, its lack of initiative. Then on November 1, a bombardment was planned. The artillery would create a "virtual curtain of steel and fire in front of the Army." Battery D was scheduled to fire 1,000 rounds. It was during this preparation that Truman again saw Harry Vaughan, who would become so important to President Truman. Vaughan later described seeing in his friend an "immovable Captain, among mud-caked soldiers, worse for wear." Battery D fired 944 high-explosive rounds in two and a half hours. They had just been officially commended for their efficiency, and they demonstrated it once more.

On October 30, Truman wrote to Bess from his Paris–Metz railroad-tunnel bunker. The army was gearing up to attack and take Fortress Metz, the mighty anchor of fortresses that France had built against a German invasion but that had fallen to the enemy. He wrote:

> You should see the place I live in. It is different from that in which I was when I wrote you last. I have a very large arched room which contains the Battery kitchen. On one side I have a small room with a stove, a table, a chair, some boxes, a lot of maps and firing tables and other necessary battery commander junk. On the other I have a sleeping compartment with room for myself and two lieutenants and a stove. The battery is up the road a couple of hundred meters and so well hidden that I can't find it myself after dark sometimes.

He always tried to be optimistic with Bess, but he was writing from the site of the imminent bloody battle at Metz.

It was another soldier, Acting Sergeant William Triplet of the 140th Infantry, at the other end of the tunnel, who left us a description of the real world around Truman and the soldiers:

> Before the war the area had been largely wooded, but an average of three shells had plowed into each three yards of soil and the low, rolling hills had been scalped of vegetation. Now and then one would see a splintered stump of the original trees, none over twelve inches high. Dugouts were everywhere over the trench lines ranging from one-man niches [dug into the trench walls] to large and commodious palaces capable of holding a section or small platoons. Some of the latter were collapsed and all badly flooded by ground seepage, unusable unless pumps kept them clear, and with rotting roof timbers that could not be trusted.

The sergeant who left this indelible description was in a company with an 86 percent casualty rate. New recruits looked at a trench of forty dead Frenchmen buried deep with only their bayonets showing. Dead in place for a year.

Truman continued in his long October 30th letter to Bess with an unusually somber note:

> I am sure that this desolate country was cultivated and beautiful like the rest of France and now, why Sahara or Arizona would look like Eden beside it. When the moon rises behind

those tree trunks I spoke of awhile ago you can imagine that the ghosts of the half-million Frenchmen who were slaughtered here are holding a sorrowful parade over the ruins. . . . Trees that were once most beautiful forest trees are stumps with naked branches sticking out making them look like ghosts. The ground is simply one mass of shell holes.

Truman was so aghast by what he found under the shell holes that, uncharacteristically, he told Bess of the gruesome sight, while trying to take the sting out of it: "There are Frenchmen buried in my front yard and Huns in the backyard and both litter up the landscape as far as you can see. Every time a Boche shell hits in a field over west of here it digs up a piece of someone. It is well I am not troubled by spooks."

The Germans were now increasing their use of gas in the Verdun area. They were using more than they had in the earlier battles Truman had experienced in the Vosges or Argonne, but Battery D was mostly spared because of careful preventive measures. One soldier reported that the Germans were now using chlorine gas, which kept close to the ground and entered tunnels. The men left their masks on. Mustard gas was also used when the weather cleared. Truman told Bess that his sleeping area was bombproof, but gas could seep in, and he slept in a gas mask. "Next time I send you a picture it will be with a gas mask on," he quipped.

On November 1, Harry described to Bess an incident that revealed a side of the American persona as well as the perceived national traits of the other combatants:

One of [the German] aviators fell right behind my Battery yesterday and sprained his ankle, busted up the machine, and got completely picked by the French and Americans in the neighborhood. They even tried to take their (there were two men in the machine) coats. One of our officers, I am ashamed to say, took the boots off the one with the sprained ankle and kept them.... I heard a Frenchman remark that Germany was fighting for territory, England for the sea, France for patriotism, and Americans for souvenirs. Yesterday made me think he was about right.

One soldier gave Truman a piece of fabric from the airplane's wing, which, decades later, he donated to his presidential library.

Truman's unit prepared to join the full Allied thrust toward the mighty Fortress Metz. A November 1 bombardment was planned for openers, providing a curtain of steel. Truman's battery was scheduled to fire hundreds of rounds. It fired 944 high-explosive rounds in two and a half hours. From October 24 to November 4, Truman's other guns laid down harassing fire, but the American troops took, then lost, their objective. Fortress Metz was held by the Germans. It was another defeat, but Truman did not tell Bess on November 10 about the shellacking. Rather, he said, without evidence: "Heine seems about finished." Then he mentioned that Battery D shot 500 rounds of high-explosive shells.

Plans were then made for another assault on November 11. But at five in the morning that day Truman got word that at 11 AM an armistice would be declared. Nevertheless, Truman fired his guns until 10:45 at a little village northeast of Verdun. To Bess he wrote that he "shot out a German Battery, shot up his big observation post, and ruined another Battery when it was moving down the road." Shells fell all around his men, making some dizzy—not him—but he "never lost a horse, nor a man." Truman praised the doughboys. As he put it: "Our infantry are the heroes of the war. There's nothing—machine guns, artillery, rifles, bayonets, mines, or anything else—that can stop them, when they start." Truman's praise for the soldiers is his clearest extant account of the finest hour of the war.

After the armistice was declared, Truman wrote to Bess, "It was so quiet it made your head ache." French soldiers were ecstatic. Truman continued in his letter that French artillerymen, full of wine, kept saluting him: "Every single one of them had to march by my bed and salute and yell, '*Vive President Wilson, Vive Captain, Artillerie American.*' No sleep all night, the infantry fired Very pistols, sent up all the flares they could lay their hands on, fired rifles, pistols and whatever else would make noise, all night long."

Truman and others were given a two-week leave to roam around France. He visited Paris and the Riviera and ventured into Italy. When he returned, his battery had gotten sloppy, and he harshly disciplined them. In his eighteen months serving his country, Truman had learned a lot about the army and war and dreamed what he would do if he were on the military affairs committee in the US Congress. He would not tolerate West Pointers' airs about how proficient they were; he would not let army officers, mostly from West Point, put down the state militias; he would not accept textbook training about static lines and not moving armies; he would accept the new artillery plan of shooting above the infantry to kill the enemy, instead of preparing the ground for infantry battles. He would give lower officers initiative to fight the war in a moving fashion, as Pershing wanted, though the general was often thwarted. Leadership was essential, but it had to be composed of intelligence, training, and initiative. Care for one's men in the command was a primary concern. Loyalty was paramount, patriotism essential, courage necessary.

At war's end, Truman put in for "full and immediate separation" from the army. The final inspection of the troops was made by General Pershing and the Prince of Wales. The general shook Truman's hand. He said, "You have a fine looking bunch of men, captain. And I hope you will take them home as clean morally and physically as they were when they came over so that the people at home can be as proud of them as I am."

Captain Truman returned home on the *Zeppelin,* landing in New York. He was twenty pounds lighter than when he had left home and Bess. He paraded through Kansas City with other returned warriors and then was discharged. He had been given a Loving Cup by his men. It was inscribed: "Captain Harry S. Truman, Presented by the members of Battery D in appreciation of his justice, ability and leadership." Truman had been recommended for a promotion to major and, again, for a commission in the regular army or reserve corps. But he was coming home to Bess, marriage, and the search for a civilian career. He certainly had no intention, and he harbored no fantasy, of going into politics.

A MAN
IN FULL

———◆◆◆———

Harry Truman was a new man when he returned home. Now 174 pounds, a bit worldly wise, a confident, courageous leader, he expected to live a middle-class life in the Middle West. During the war, in a December 14, 1918, letter from the battlefield, he had outlined his ideal life to Bess:

> I've almost come to the conclusion that it's not intended for me ever to be very rich, nor very poor, and I am about convinced that that will be about the happiest state a man can be. To have the finest girl in all the whole world (and to make the statement without fear of contradiction) to share my joys and troubles, mostly joys I'm hoping, to have just enough of this world's goods to make it pleasant to try for more, to own a Ford and tour the U.S.A. and France perhaps . . . and still have a nice little country home to be comfortable in—well that's really not a hard fortune to contemplate. Maybe have a little

FIGURE 9 Wedding photo of Harry and Bess Truman, June 28, 1919, in the backyard of 219 N. Delaware, Independence, Missouri. *Credit:* Harry S. Truman Library.

politics and some nice little dinner parties occasionally just for good measure. How does it sound to you? Just its contemplation has almost cured me of the blues.

Before he came home, Harry had been to Italy and cities in France—Paris, Nice, Marseilles. He had dined at Maxim's, saw all the great tourist sites, including low dives, and went to the opera while friends gambled at casinos. He was no rube returning to America. The offhanded mention of politics seems anomalous and enigmatic.

Harry Truman, thirty-five, and Bess Wallace, thirty-four, were married on June 28, 1919, at Trinity Episcopal Church in Independence. It was a ceremony of understated elegance. The groom wore a fine tailored suit and the bride a dress of white georgette and a hat of white faille. She carried a small bouquet of roses. Music was by Felix Mendelssohn and Charles Gounod. Harry placed the wedding ring on Bess's finger. He had bought it in Paris, just before sailing home. They spent their honeymoon in Chicago, Detroit, and Port Huron Beach, Michigan, traveling in Harry's new Dodge roadster. They then settled in Bess's mother's house at 219 North Delaware Street, in Independence. The next three years were a year of happiness and two of distress.

Truman was a full representative of the Midwest, a still-dominant nineteenth-century culture. He was never a part of the Jazz Age, gin-drinking, avant-garde-crazed, selfish, anything-goes culture. He retained his steady, energetic, agreeable nature. These qualities, honed by the war, were his most successful accomplishments. He became a take-charge man, a leader, a confident not-quite middle-aged man. He claimed that he had in his pocket his final pay as a captain, a $60 bonus ($795 in today's dollars), and money to return home, all of which he was spending. It was a help that he moved into the Gates house with no expenses. But at what psychic cost? It was a compound: a large house in which Bess's grandmother Gates lived, possibly on the first floor, as she was very old and disabled; there was a master bedroom upstairs where his mother-in-law, the real matriarch, slept. Harry and Bess had a smaller bedroom, and the youngest Wallace son had a room. Outside, there were two bungalows for the other two Wallace brothers and their wives. Dinners were somewhat formal and served in the main house, with a cook in the kitchen. Harry sat at one end of the table and Mrs. Wallace at the other. We don't know whether Harry was the head or the foot. Only sixty years later did a Truman family member say that Harry actually liked his accommodations. That opinion was probably based on his and Bess's getting the master bedroom when old Mrs. Gates died, as the matriarch herself had become disabled and needed the first-floor bedroom. Truman kept a business address in Kansas City. When Bess traveled, he took a room in a hotel or stayed with his family at the Grandview farm. There may be a message there to counter the story of his liking his domestic accommodations. He and Bess had Sunday dinner with his family, which she is reported to have enjoyed.

Harry's finances for the first few years of his marriage fell into three categories: the family farm in Grandview, his old business deals, and a haberdashery store. As always, they were sources of emotional stress for not just Harry but also Bess. And it cannot be insignificant that Bess suffered two miscarriages in these early years, but we have no letters or evidence of their causes or meaning. Finally, however, Mary Margaret, always called Margaret, was born in 1924. Bess wrote to Harry that she was sorry she bore a girl because she thought he wanted a boy. Truman demurred, for his love and devotion to Margaret were extraordinary, and grew over the years.

The Truman farm and landholdings had to be unscrambled and dissolved. Mamma Truman and Mary Jane ran a prosperous, rented-out farm. Old Mrs. Truman was as tough as ever, still hunting rabbits with a 16-gauge shotgun. Harry's brother, Vivian, ran a sixty-five-acre farm, which had come to him from Uncle Harrison's estate. Now, Harrison's herd of pigs was sold for $4,000. Everything else was sold for $15,000, with Harry getting around one-third from the sale. He had told Bess that he had a debt of $1,000 in early 1918. After the sale, Harry owned nothing of the land Uncle Harrison had left him. The family was heavily in debt. Mary Jane owed $52,000; Vivian, $2,100; Martha, $31,200. Harry got involved and failed to sell his mother's farm for $50,000. Then fifty-five acres were broken off for building lots, and Mamma carried some of the mortgages. Harry took $2,700 to pay off some of his debts. Martha succeeded in halving her debt, but not until 1932 did she sell off the remaining lots.

Beyond Harry's farm problems was his attachment to his prewar oil interest and to the Morgan Company, a new firm that was part in oil and part in brokerage. In 1918, he might have gained $1,000 from this old deal. What these two interests and the farm meant was that when he married Bess he had no discoverable, steady source of income. He persevered. In December 1920, Truman's Morgan partner transferred to Harry a large Kansas City house with an $8,500 mortgage. Harry now got out of the oil and brokerage businesses and went into real estate. He traded the Kansas City house for a three-story apartment building with mortgages totaling $17,600. A partner took two-thirds of the mortgages. Truman then swapped his apartment interest for a 160-acre farm in Johnson County, Kansas, with two mortgages totaling $8,800. Truman estimated his equity stake at $5,000, the total purchase being $13,800. He ambled along, economically on edge. The details of his finances are mind-boggling.

Harry's great success so far had been in the war. So in the 1920s, as he went from one business failure to the next, the citizen soldier eagerly participated in military groups. Gregarious and likeable, he made lifelong friendships in these organizations. A major dimension of Truman's life from 1920 to 1935 that ran parallel to his various occupations was his involvement in voluntary organizations and the Army Reserve. Having good connections was a part of the business ethos of the 1920s. One cannot understand his plunging economic entrepreneurship without factoring in these avocations. He held memberships in more than a dozen organizations and when he joined the Army Reserves, later called the Organized Reserve Corps, he made more friends for life. He was gregarious, well-liked, and was attracted to male companionship. He was a serious soldier citizen

FIGURE 10 *Left to right:* Harry Vaughan, Harry S. Truman, and John W. Snyder, in their Army Reserve Officer uniforms, ca. 1936. *Credit:* Harry S. Truman Library.

and even joined the American Legion. By 1923 the Army Reserves were training for two weeks every year with the National Guard. Over the years, Truman trained at Forts Leavenworth and Riley in Kansas, Camp Ripley in Minnesota, and Camp Pike in Arkansas. He became a lieutenant colonel in 1925 and colonel in 1932. He reconnected with his old army buddy Harry Vaughan, who would become President Truman's military aide. And he met the future hero of Bataan, Jonathan Wainwright.

Social and military connections were essential to a successful business life, Truman believed, and in this he was not unlike the eponymous hero of Sinclair Lewis's 1922 satirical novel *Babbitt*, who became a famous symbol of middle-class conformism. Harry's social clubs included the Masons, the Triangle

Club of young businessmen, the National Old Trails Club, the elite Kansas City Club, and the Lakewood Country Club. Marrying Bess and being a member of elite clubs signaled a rise in his social status. It is a puzzlement why, with all these connections, he did not succeed in business.

Truman's social bubble burst when his third postwar major enterprise failed. But it was the recession of the early 1920s that did him in. With a partner, he had opened a high-level haberdashery store. On May 17, 1919, with an army buddy, Eddie Jacobson, Truman signed a five-year lease, at $350 a month, for a store in a good downtown site in Kansas City. The farmer, miner, oil executive, money broker, soldier, realtor was now a city merchant of snazzy accoutrements for men—$16 silk shirts, underwear, collars, belts, gloves, hats. No suits. The store opened in November 1919. Expenses were high: $1,050 for advance rent and $6,835.82 for fixtures, inventory, and ads. Their debt was $5,000. Truman put up $4,000. Jacobson, nothing! Jacobson knew the business; Harry kept the books. The partners worked very hard from 8 AM to 9 PM and took only a weekly salary of $40 each. The business seemed prosperous. Then the recession of 1921 hit all businesses hard, and Truman & Jacobson Haberdashery was in trouble. The partners decided to incorporate and probably raised $12,000. The next year was dismal and there were "no purchasers." Debts mounted to $13,000.

In September 1922, the partners closed their doors. Their store had been weakly capitalized and could not compete with larger, similar businesses. Truman had made a big and expensive entrepreneurial mistake. Clearly, his record shows that he was

FIGURE 11 Harry S. Truman in the clothing store he and Eddie Jacobson owned, ca. 1920. Truman & Jacobson Haberdashery was located at 12th and Baltimore (104 West 12th), Kansas City, Missouri. The store opened in 1919 and failed in 1922. *Left to right:* Harry Truman, Francis Berry, Mike Flynn, and Kelsey Cravens. *Credit:* Harry S. Truman Library.

not, and never would be, a successful businessman. He settled with his creditors. But his bank debt was another matter, and the bank wanted its money. Truman had borrowed $2,500. The bank extracted some money from Truman's farm. In a convoluted deal, the bank sold the Truman farm and gave Truman $1,043.58 and issued a debt for $6,261.44. Legal actions about Harry's and his mother's debts went on for years, the debt growing to $8,944.78. Truman paid off some debt via mortgages held by his mother with property as collateral and, over two years, paid off the balance with the sale of another lot from his mother's land. It was almost a Dickensian tale. Only in 1935 was the debt cleared when Vivian gave the bank $1,000. Jacobson declared bankruptcy in 1925. Truman refused such a solution. Why? For any future occupation he calculated that he needed an ethical financial record.

Once more in debt and jobless, Truman looked on a landscape of gloom and despair. He had failed again. Could he summon up his courage to try again? We don't know if he suffered existential angst, because letters between Bess and Harry are almost nonexistent for this period, since they were together most of the time. We should also recall that Bess in later years burned her letters and some of Harry's from this painful time. When many years later Margaret Truman—some say it was Harry himself—saw Bess throwing letters into the fire, she, or Harry, tried to stop her with the words, "Think of posterity." Bess retorted, "I am."

Because Truman had sometimes mentioned the possibility of going into politics, he now became a student of this possibility. He would be open to running for office, something that was mentioned to Harry by his Pendergast army buddy when Harry was a haberdasher and prosperous. He had a business, and did not think of closing it to be a politician. But he was bemused. When Truman & Jacobson failed, Harry got interested in what would become his final, and first successful, profession. When he made this momentous decision and was asked why, he quipped: "I have to eat."

Politics in Jackson County and Kansas City was a closed system, run by a machine with a powerful boss, who was only sometimes challenged. At this time in American politics, there were two kinds of political machines. One directed downward with a strong boss and minions at levels; the other, more democratic, with power rising up to a boss. Jackson County and Kansas City belonged to the first type, although the City was not a part of the County. The Pendergast machine was probably the most powerful political organization in the country. There were others: Boston, Cleveland, Tammany Hall in New York City, Mayor Frank "I Am the Law" Hague in Jersey City. The one embracing Truman was arguably the most powerful, corrupt, and violent of the famous machines. It was run by Tom Pendergast, uncle of Jim Pendergast, Truman's army buddy. Jim was the son of Mike Pendergast and nephew of Big Jim, the late founder of one of the two factions in Kansas City's Democratic Party. The party had long had two warring factions, so rich were the spoils of politics.

Young Jim had been a battery commander in the war—Battery A, 130th Field Artillery regiment. Truman admired his fellow battery commanders, who had served with honor, as he had. In 1921, Harry's and Jim's paths crossed again at a raucous American Legion convention, and they bonded. The men were members of the warrior caste. The next year, Jim's father, Mike, asked Harry to run for the position of eastern judge on the Jackson County court, an administrative position with great power over appropriations for roads, bridges, buildings, and so on. Harry's Democratic faction engaged in a bruising war with the opposing Democratic faction. His side needed an honest, down-to-earth, non-politician, war-veteran candidate. Truman fit the bill and seized his opportunity.

What was he getting into? He was a novice, both to politics and to the particularly venomous battles that scarred the Democratic Party. Jackson County, Missouri—unlike wide-open Kansas City—was a quintessential nineteenth-century rural area of Protestants, old families, farm folk of simple habits, and independence. Kansas City was the antithesis: a smaller Chicago. It was highly immigrant, with a Jazz Age morality. And Tom Pendergast was the kingpin, the Boss. He owned and controlled through every means necessary saloons, wards, gambling, illegal liquor, brothels, and even the police, who took orders from him. It was a truism, then and now, although always rejected by politicians, that you cannot have crime without the police knowing about it. Be that as it may, there were a few positive things, to be sure, that the Kansas City machine accomplished, like building a stunning art nouveau railroad terminal, Union Station, and engaging in small philanthropies to the poor—turkeys at Christmas and coal in the winter. But Pendergast's grasping patronage and skimming of money from jobs he doled out (called lugs), contracts, and illegal activities were legendary. Pendergast lived large and lavishly at public expense. He was a masterly power broker and organizer, well known in the nation's politics.

When Truman tiptoed into this degradation of democracy in 1922, he entered a new world, whose working parts he could only slowly understand. He had to accommodate himself to a situation that was the obverse of his mother's deep-seated teaching of ethical behavior, no matter the circumstances. As we trace Truman's activities during his two, non-contiguous terms as county judge, two aspects will interest us: first, what was the psychic cost to this hitherto honest man in a den of thieves, and second, what did he accomplish of lasting value, despite the political sleaze he was enmeshed in? During this time, Truman was plagued with serious psychosomatic disorders. They disabled him, often for days, and he would disappear, hiding out in hotels. During these episodes, he would write down what was going on, and we luckily have those notes, called The Pickwick Papers, for the hotel he most often fled to.

The accomplishments were impressive. He had been personally courageous at the outset of his political career, winning the judgeship by 282 votes, while defying the Ku Klux Klan, which threatened to kill him after he attacked them in a speech. He had the soldier vote, and his buddies protected him with shotguns in their cars, ready for any eventuality.

Truman became a trustee of his budding career and historian of his affairs when he penned and published a remarkable book on regional planning, still available, that explained his stewardship of Jackson County, although he did not put his name as author on the volume. The book merely stated: "Leader in plan activities was Harry S. Truman, presiding judge of the County Court." Entitled *Results of County Planning: Jackson County Missouri,* the book, highly illustrated, with elegant, long captions, is good reading even today. It stressed the need for roads to market crops, based on practical needs and not politics, and the ways to enjoy the natural beauty of the area. Bond issues of about $10,000,000 were spent, the best engineers were hired, and 166 miles of concrete roads and 52 miles of secondary roads were built. The plan had an inner belt highway circling Kansas City and an outer belt highway circling the remote parts of the county, with connecting links. There was no grid pattern, but winding roads to show off the beauty of the area, the historic houses, the new and handsome bridges, and the schools, including orphanages for black children. Truman waxed poetic on almost every page: "Through miniature canyons, many of Jackson County's most scenic highways wander, every now and then the traveler coming upon distant views of finest natural landscaping. Everywhere are trees and foliage . . . and welcome shade from summer sun."

The book showed the new courthouses that Truman spent so much time on, traveling by car, at his own expense, to view other states' courthouses, first hand, to garner ideas. He wound up building one courthouse in Federal style and another in Art Deco style. Truman spearheaded the Greater Kansas City Regional Plan Association and became its first president. Six counties were included, and plans were on the drawing board for recreation and parks not unlike what Frederick Law Olmstead had created in the Boston area, an emerald necklace. Truman was the most energetic and farseeing county judge in the county's history. His burst of building and planning remade the area and only stopped when he was elected to the US Senate, with new responsibilities, in 1934.

Truman's local career is seen by historians in the larger context of history that downplays his provincial accomplishments.

FIGURE 12 Jackson County Judge Harry S. Truman signing county checks
with a multiple machine, September 24, 1927. *Credit: Kansas City Journal
Post,* courtesy of the Harry S. Truman Library.

Truman kept ties to Pendergast. He was the Boss's representative in the eastern district. Truman himself left us a reminis-
cence: "I controlled the Democratic Party in eastern Jackson
County when I was county judge.... In any election I could de-
liver 11,000 votes and not steal one. It was not necessary. I
looked out for people and they understood leadership." In the
Kansas City Star it was reported both in 1926 and 1930 of Truman that there was "not a suspicion of graft."

The Pickwick Papers, however, detail a hidden political life.
In them, Truman admits that he was forced to let a former saloon
keeper steal $10,000 from county revenues. He wrote that, at
another time, $1,000,000 was stolen. Pendergast was besieged
by his men looking for contracts from Truman to build roads
and structures. He told them Truman was "the hardheadest,

orniest man in the world; there isn't anything I can do. . . . You get your price right and get the best material. You heard him say it; you'll get the business." In the $50,000,000 in bonds ready for bid, Truman had told the bidders that he wanted the best materials, engineering, and estimates. The lowest bid with the highest-quality materials would get the job. We are left with a double record of Truman's early political life, one of a man torn between behaving ethically and having to be minimally corrupt. There was no way he could advertise his fight for honesty. Outwardly, he pointed to his deeds; inwardly, he left a secret record of exculpation.

Truman was holding fast at the same time that newspapers were reporting that there was direct corruption elsewhere. In Kansas City, in 1932, the police department, which the state had given over to local control, had a 10 percent enrollment of men with criminal records. At one point, a daughter of an official was kidnapped, but not for long. This was, as yet, beyond the pale. In 1934, violence in elections was the standard as "gangs of political machine goons drove around in automobiles without license plates." The worst was in Kansas City, under Pendergast's thumb. One newspaper wrote, "If you want to see some sin, forget about Paris and go to Kansas City . . . probably . . . the greatest sin industry in the world." Pendergast is reported to have told Truman that in Kansas City every bid for contracting was distorted so "an insider gentleman got the contract." Truman wrote that—despite debilitating illnesses recorded in his Pickwick Hotel stays (severe headaches, stomach trouble, and such)—he had saved $1,000,000 in Jackson

County business, and $3,500,000 through his honest bidding program. At one point in his Pickwick writing, he calculated that he, himself, could have picked up $1,500,000 if he had been dishonest. He chose not to be. All his life, he remained a virtually, and virtuously, poor man, only the surprising presidency finally giving him a good living.

Only later, and when Truman had moved on, was it determined that $11,000,000 was missing from Kansas City managers' accounts. Kansas City was Pendergast's honey pot. Truman, however, was known to give some jobs to "deserving Democrats," that is, Pendergast men. Still, he maintained a high reputation for honesty. His bowing to the Boss was minimal, as the Pickwick Papers show. The best Truman account of how he mediated between his troubled conscience and his misdeeds is in his own hand in the Pickwick Papers: "I wonder if I did right to put a lot of no account sons of bitches on the payroll and pay other sons of bitches more money for supplies than they were worth in order to satisfy the political powers and save $3,500,000."

It was only years later that Truman realized that Pendergast's Kansas City machine was as hellishly corrupt as others in New York City, Cincinnati, Jersey City, Chicago, Los Angeles, San Francisco, and Pittsburgh. It should be mentioned, as at least one scholar does, that even though Truman's eastern district was not in Kansas City, he was as much a Kansas City politician as Pendergast. Most probably this harsh judgment is based on the fact that there is no written record that Truman ever disconnected himself from Pendergast. And he later attended the

Boss's funeral when he was vice president. Would Truman have been as successful in winning office if he had decided to join with Pendergast's adversaries in the Democratic Party, who were also crooked? Was it even possible not to bend in politics when Pendergast ruled? Not even history can lead to a conclusion. Truman himself, in the Pickwick Papers, left a kind of psychological justification for why he was a Pendergast man. "I am obliged to the Big Boss, a man of his word; but he gives it very seldom and only on a sure thing. But he's not a trimmer. He, in past times, owned a bawdy house, a saloon and gambling establishment, was raised in that environment but he's all man." How manliness overrode honesty boggles the mind.

That Truman was not corrupt enough is shown by his loss in 1924 as county judge. That was the only election Truman ever lost. Too many votes were lost in Jackson County, as one faction of the Democratic Party refused to back him. Two years before, the triumphant Truman had given the game away when he said that when they won they took all the jobs—there were none for adversaries.

After he lost in 1924, Harry got a job with the American Automobile Association selling subscriptions. He was successful, earning about $5,000 a year, but it was boring; then ruffians helped the Boss retake the party and in 1926 Truman returned to power. He was now presiding county judge, that is, a kind of president. Pendergast was at the height of his power in doling out jobs, everything from laborers to judges, to congressmen and US senators. Even when Kansas City wrote a new charter and held a special election, Pendergast managed to manipulate the machinery, in the face of the Republican opposition, to control events, even to dictate who became the Kansas City manager, the city's chief administrator. In their richly detailed book *Pendergast,* Lawrence A. Larson and Nancy H. Hudson conclude about Truman in 1926:

> His great organizational ability, combined with the help of criminal elements, the acquiescence of the business community, the emphasis on votes rather than ideology, and the use of ruthless tactics, created the powerful Pendergast Machine.... Would he or did he want to escape from his criminal and gambling connections? Was he, no matter the façade, simply a thug who had made good in politics?

Tom Pendergast had a luxurious lifestyle, lived in a mansion, traveled to Europe like a prince, and was driven about in high-end cars. His children went to private schools. Truman never met the Boss's family or visited his French Regency–Italian Renaissance–style place, furnished with Louis XV reproductions. The election victory of 1926 simply thrust Truman back into his double life. The margins for victories that year were about 50,000 votes in each of the major elections. It was the time of the passage of the $10 million bond issues and the high tide of Truman's legendary building programs.

In 1928, Pendergast established his most successful business, the Ready Mixed Concrete Company. He had a hand in the building industry in Kansas City—outside of Truman's jurisdiction—and owned about twenty businesses, including insurance firms. Other kinds of businesses paid regular tribute to him—anywhere from 5 to 10 percent of profits—and local police powers—regulatory, taxes, and licensing—were under machine control. One Republican leader exclaimed about Pendergast in a Kansas City election campaign in 1930: "Like the grand Army of Napoleon supported by the conquered nations of Europe, it sets forth in this campaign, banners waving and bands playing, in its march to Moscow."

In 1932, Pendergast, in charge of Missouri's delegation to the Democratic National Convention, threw his votes to Franklin D. Roosevelt. The country was in the third year of the worst depression in its history. Roosevelt promised a New Deal, a time of experiment to get the economy moving and promote jobs. His programs, at first, were not what he is remembered for on the domestic side—he would balance the budget, for example, and proposed a National Recovery Act, which would join employers and employees together to revive business. The latter was a failure; the former, soon abandoned. But he closed the banks to give them time to reset themselves and prevent more people from taking out their money and causing bankruptcies. He separated commercial from investment banking to protect small depositors. Mostly, he was not Herbert Hoover and promised hope and action. Truman was a Roosevelt supporter from habit as a Democrat and for the promises an administration by him would bring: hope and change. Later, of course, there would be momentous programs like Social Security for retirees; the Agricultural Adjustment Administration for farmers, which raised prices; the Civilian

Conservation Corps for jobless youth, while helping to conserve the environment; the Public Works Administration, which built bridges, tunnels, and infrastructure; an act to legalize unions, and so on. There was no way Truman or Pendergast in 1932 could have foreseen the bonanza of jobs and money that would soon pour into states and localities because of these New Deal programs. But the promise was bright, and the two men were eager to support the man who pledged to banish fear and get the country moving again. Roosevelt would become the father of the welfare state, a new turn in politics that had already blossomed abroad in Germany and England in the late nineteenth and early twentieth centuries. Laissez faire, with its booms and busts, was discredited.

Truman immediately received some spoils, as he was appointed national reemployment director for the state, while retaining his judgeship. Pendergast, meanwhile, ran the Civil Works Administration in Missouri, which employed 100,000 men to build infrastructure. Truman helped the Boss run the machine and was made vice president of the Jackson Democratic Club. Six thousand members each paid $6 in weekly dues. Truman was one of six sub-bosses, at election time, when half of their patronage salaries were paid to the machine. In another Pendergast practice, voters swung to Pendergast if they wanted city services. Assessments in property also followed elections. Friends were well treated, adversaries punished. New Deal make-work programs funneled monies from jobholders to the machine coffers. Truman was still known for his independence and was never accused of using any office for personal gain. He always said he entered office poor and left poor. This is a true statement, as there is no evidence of his living high, or even buying his own home, in Pendergast's heyday.

In private, in his Pickwick Papers, Truman thundered against corrupt officeholders by name and, in a rare instance, also attacked churchgoers who were a part of the ongoing hypocrisy. In one of his many salty statements he wrote in his secret memos: "Who is to blame for present conditions but sniveling church members who weep on Sunday, play with whores on Monday, drink on Tuesday, sell out to the Boss on Wednesday, repent about Friday and start over on Sunday.... I think, maybe the Boss is nearer to heaven than the snivelers." Truman's divided conscience once more led him to displaced anger. He could despise himself when he had to be dishonest but blamed the system.

Pendergast's 1930s decade, when he presided over the widest-open city in the country, grossed about $32,000,000 a year from every kind of criminal activity and political contributions. He added to his empire unclothed waitresses in nightclubs. Kansas City, meanwhile, became the Midwest's drug distribution center. And the Mafia and its boss Johnny Lazia had a foot in the door with all the evils it represented. Pendergast used a part of Lazia's outfit to collect corrupt monies, slug poll workers, create rackets that netted him millions of dollars, and make appointments of felons to the police department. Lazia protected in Kansas City high-profile criminals from other states and staged massacres. He was convicted of tax evasion and sent to jail. Pendergast interceded with Postmaster

General James Farley, Roosevelt's patronage boss, to reach into the judicial system to get Lazia off. Only the assassination of Lazia in July 1934 ended this sordid affair. In retrospect, Pendergast was a white-collar criminal, not a Murder Incorporated type, and was always uneasy about the Mafia intrusion into his cozy, corrupt world. He paid his respects at Lazia's funeral and resumed his "normal" activities.

When a reformer in 1932 spoke to the Government Study Club in Kansas City, he castigated members by declaring: "You have turned your City over to a gang and given it into the hands of crooks and racketeers because you are asleep." Ensuing threats on the speaker's life and on state and federal grand juries scared off reform and merely put the Boss's machine on the defensive. Pendergast denied wrongdoing in the press, the police lied about crime, and little changed.

Truman was on the horns of a dilemma. In his Pickwick Papers, he called one officeholder "a crook of the worst water" and speculated that another "stole a half million dollars as a county judge." But he thought Kansas City was less corrupt than other large cities and named them. He blamed the larger society rather than the men in power. It was a remarkable act of denial. To record in private, probably about Jackson County, that "we have an extraordinary clean local government" was mostly true. His relative personal honesty among the thieves did not protect his body, however, which rebelled into psychosomatic illnesses, calibrated to the tightness of his ties to Pendergast. Only as they loosened would he get better, but that time was yet to come.

There are references all through Truman's letters to Bess about his illnesses and psychic distress. On February 12, 1931, he mentions "the tremendous amount of strain.... I either had to run away or go on a big drunk." Even from Fort Riley, Kansas, he writes in August 1931: "I had an accommodation spasm ... beside a headache." April 8, 1933: "I was sick last night ... and lost my supper. I have to go off and hide. I am now on the seventh floor of the Pickwick Hotel. The manager gave me a room without registering. No job holder who wants to stay on can see or phone me." On May 9 he wrote that his job "is sometimes hard on head and nerves." At another time, away from politics while at Camp Pike with reservists, he happily wrote that he was in "perfect health, no headache, and no dizziness."

Truman wandered about in the Pickwick Papers with some bizarre statements that showcase his mind. In 1931, no date found, he wrote that he hoped for a "reformation of the heart [sic] teach our kids honor and kill a few sex symbols [unclear] to put boys in High schools to themselves with *men* teachers (not sissies)." He wished to "close all the girls finishing schools, shoot all the efficiency experts and become a nation of God's people once more." In hiding, he was blowing off steam and displacing his anger. He knew the Bible from his mother's teachings, had joined the Baptist Church as a young man, and was not averse to calling on a god of vengeance from the Old Testament, not the forgiving god of the New Testament. In the Pickwick Papers in May 1931, he reminisced: "Mike Pendergast picked me up and put me into politics and I've been lucky. I'm still an idealist and I still believe that Jehovah will reward the righteous and punish the wrongdoers. . . . Have tried to make Jackson County's government ideal as far as the practical operation will allow. . . . Oh if I were only John D. [Rockefeller] or [Andrew] Mellon or [abolitionist] Wendell Phillips, I'd make this section (six counties) the world's real paradise. What's the use of wishing. I'm still going to do it."

On May 7, 1933, anticipating his forty-ninth birthday the next day, Truman wrote to Bess and seemed somewhat content with his life: "Take it all together . . . the experience has been worthwhile. I'd like to do it again. I've been in a railroad, bank, farm, war, politics, *love* . . . been busted and yet I have stayed an idealist. . . . Politics should make a thief, a roué, and a pessimist of anyone but I don't believe I am any of them." Truman surely knew he had feet of clay, but to admit it might destroy him and his family. His distress would make him a sick and useless breadwinner for his large, extended family.

Indeed, Harry needed to provide for his family. He thought of becoming county collector, with the handsome salary of $10,000 a year, but Pendergast said no. He thought of running for Congress, but the Boss didn't support that either. Truman had given Tom Pendergast so much trouble by not allowing corrupt contracts, he wrote in the Pickwick Papers, that he could only assume that Pendergast did not want an honest man in some positions. The Boss's graft would decrease, and the rich life he led would be diminished. Truman then thought of running for governor but again the Boss said no. So what was Pendergast going to do with an "honest" politician? The answer: Kick him out of state and upstairs. Truman would run for US

Senate, which was farther from patronage and spoils that came to the state through federal programs and not to men in elective federal office. There would be other candidates who wanted the Senate seat, but Truman would have to run on his record with little help from the Boss. Truman thought his name would not be linked with the "misdeeds and misfortunes of Pendergast." He honestly believed that he had an unblemished record as a public servant. He thought his accomplishments were obvious and well known. He was wrong of course, but that is ahead of our story. Truman's position as presiding county judge would be his last local job. He was taking a big chance in going for the Senate seat. He opined: "I will be a pauper when I am done." That is, if he gave up a sure thing for a glittering prize. Because he never took bribes, he asked himself whether he was "a fool or ethical giant." So far, he was a "small duck in a very large puddle." But he had been safe. Could he master the rushing waters of an ocean? Could he rise from a county official to federal office?

Truman intended to take running for the Senate very seriously. Every ounce of his energy would go into the campaigns, first in a primary and then in the general election. He traveled the state in his own car and made up to ten visits a day to towns and crossroads. He shook hands with 100,000 people. He was not charismatic or a good speaker. He read from texts and was not spontaneous. He was short and trim, with a sharp nose. He was well-dressed and wore a hat. No newspapers took him seriously or paid him much attention. As it turned out, he won the primary with machine help. He garnered 276,850 votes to others' 236,105 and 147,614. He went on to win the election with 787,110 votes to 524,954.

With Truman headed to DC, the Pendergast machine jumped in to reap any new rewards with New Deal jobs. The Works Progress Administration alone had 80,000 jobs available for Missouri. Truman responded to all job seekers with the words: "If you will send us endorsements from the Kansas City Democratic organization, I shall be glad to do what I can for you." One did not need to be a genius to know what that meant. Soon, the machine was awash with jobs with, undoubtedly, the usual lug that came with such positions. Earlier, Truman, as head of the Federal Relief Administration in Missouri, an unpaid position, was so disenchanted by the invisible strings attached to such a job that he wrote to Bess on January 1, 1934, that he did not care as much for the position "as I thought I was going to. There'll be almost as many rocks heaved at me as there are now." This program gave cash to poor families whose breadwinner had lost his job; it really saved the American family. Most probably Pendergast had engineered giving the post to Truman, whose reputation for honesty was surely better than the Boss's in Washington. But he had taken it only for a while, and now, as senator, the patronage flood would be at full tide.

Now that he was going to Washington, another problem loomed for the Trumans. Bess was not in favor of living in Washington, away from her mother. But she came to the nation's capital, with her husband and their daughter. They moved into a four-room apartment for $150 a month—a high rent in those days—and Truman borrowed money for furniture and a rented piano. It was Bess's plan to join Harry for half the year, when the Congress was in session, and to spend half back home with her mother. When Congress stayed longer, Harry moved into a hotel, alone. Margaret shuttled between schools in two cities. He and Margaret adored each other, and he missed his "baby." She was fragile, and when she got sick, he sent Bess and "baby" to Florida. Bess and Harry could never resolve the co- nundrum of their domestic needs with Mrs. Wallace's. Bess would never choose Harry over her mother in organizing their lives. When Mrs. Wallace was later disabled, they took her to Washington with them, and she shared the second bedroom, in whatever apartment Harry found for them—they moved every year—with Margaret. In later years, when Truman was president, he begged Bess to join him all year, he was so lonely, living in the "great white jail," as he called the White House. She was unmoved. Her grandson writes that she loved being a sen- ator's wife. Yet, she seemed, really, to hate Washington and the cave dwellers (the old-time socialites) who made fun of her seersucker dresses.

When Truman became a candidate for the Senate, he left us his promise: "I am going to pray as King Solomon did for wis- dom to do the job." He would need the wisdom of Solomon in the years to come.

CHAPTER 4

MAVERICK
NEW DEALER

arry Truman entered the Senate in January 1935, between the ruins of the First New Deal and the next, spec-
tacular, Second New Deal. Congress was controlled by the
Democratic Party, and President Roosevelt paid Senator Truman no mind. Harry found that he was not welcomed into the
Senate. He suffered all the poisoned arrows from his origins in
politics. The *New York Times* couldn't believe his election. It
even misnamed him Henry and called him "a rube from Pendergast land." Others said he was the Senator from Pendergast.
Some of his colleagues never considered him a senator. One
thought of him as "poison" and refused to speak to him. A po-
tential aide would not work for him as he thought Truman was
sent to Washington by "gangsters." The new senator would need
a thick skin and a soldier's courage to survive these days. But
he had gained confidence in his abilities from the army and politics and thought that he could show his mettle quickly with his

diligence. He would be a workhorse and not a show horse in that august body. There were not too many of the former and far too many of the latter.

The senator's first term slides from one depiction that could be titled "The Invisible Senator" to a second dubbed "The Senator Is Noticed." It would not be wrong to call most of these years a failure because other senators generally ignored him, the story getting around that he "had calluses on his ears taking long distance calls from Kansas City." For example, the president and his administration overlooked him when it doled out the patronage to the senior senator, Bennett Clark. Jobs and monies to Missouri flowed through Clark's office. But Truman himself sabotaged his early reputation by defending Pendergast in a Senate speech.

Other senators overlooked Truman's impressive Democratic win by 40,000 votes in the election and his popularity at home for his good works in developing Jackson County. He continually complained about the loaves and fishes distribution of patronage, for he knew well that jobs glued the party together. He found the president "unreliable." South Carolina Senator Jimmy Byrnes, who was very close to the president and was later an important Truman friend, overlooked the newcomer. Truman thought "jobs should not interfere with principles," an odd statement given his trials by fire as a Pendergast acolyte. But what kind of a faithful New Dealer could the administration expect, given their scorn?

Truman was put on the Appropriations Committee and the Committee on Interstate Commerce, two major committees, and on three minor ones, Public Buildings and Grounds, Printing, and the District of Columbia. The last was so distasteful that he asked to be excused. Only later was he put on a Military Affairs subcommittee. He was a silent committee member, mostly, in his early years, almost a fish out of water because he held in his head the last words Pendergast left with him: "Work hard, keep your mouth shut and answer your mail." But he tried, at least, to look senatorial, for when he was sworn in, he wore a morning coat and striped pants. Similar sartorial splendor began at the nation's beginnings, and Harry followed protocol. He would not look like a country hick. He wanted to fit in. To be successful, Truman knew one had to respond to constituents' needs as revealed in letters to their senators. Whether they voted to re-elect would depend on their senator bringing home the bacon.

The Senate had sixty-nine Democrats and twenty-seven Republicans; the majority party could do what it wanted. Truman made some acquaintances among that majority—mostly from the Midwest and West; easterners and southerners were scarce. These included Carl Hatch of New Mexico, Lewis Schwellenbach of Washington, Burton K. Wheeler of Montana, and Carl Hayden of Arizona. He got to know the Republicans Arthur Vandenberg of Michigan and William E. Borah of Idaho. He particularly liked John Nance Garner of Texas, the poker-playing, bourbon-drinking, cigar-smoking vice president. A good student of the Boss, Truman worked hard, arriving at 7:30 in the morning at his office, and made sure he answered his mail. He doled out the few jobs at his disposal, including one to brother Vivian and another to a friend, Ted Marks, from his army days. Later, he added his sister, Mary Jane, to his office payroll back home at $1,800 a year, and put Bess on his Washington staff at $2,400 a year. By that time Madge Wallace, his mother-in-law, was living with the Trumans in their small Washington apartment, and he was also supporting four families and two houses on his senatorial salary of $10,000 a year and Bess's salary. He kept to his personal pledge of never taking money in office, even if that meant he stayed poor. A few dollars from the Masons for public addresses helped somewhat.

The Boss's third rule, to keep your mouth shut, Truman broke after four months in office, when the silent senator introduced his first bill, to provide insurance by the Farm Credit Administration to mortgages on farm property. He was very sensitive to farm issues during the Great Depression, when, for example, the price of a dozen eggs fell from twenty-five cents to five cents and 18,000 farmers in Missouri alone were foreclosed. The mortgage on his mother's farm was overdue and was in danger of foreclosure. The nation was still heavily agrarian, although industry boomed in the late nineteenth century. But the Congress had trouble knowing how to help farmers, and Truman's bill died at birth. Roosevelt had stepped up in May 1933 with his Agricultural Adjustment Act, which raised prices through scarcity, and things improved for farmers.

These early years for Truman were a time of great reforms by Congress, with bills like the Wagner-Connery Act of 1935, which upheld the right of employees to join labor organizations, and programs like the Works Progress Administration (WPA), which built infrastructure and provided 8.5 million jobs and spent $11 billion, until it was discontinued in 1943. Over 651,000 miles of highways were built and almost 250,000 bridges, public buildings, parks, and airports built or renovated. It also gave work to artists, writers, actors, and musicians under its broad mandate. The WPA spawned the Public Works Administration, the Civilian Conservation Corps, and the National Youth Administration (Lyndon Johnson, the future president, was head of the Texas NYA). Other major New Deal laws were the Social Security Act of 1935, unemployment compensation, and the Public Utility Holding Company Act, which counteracted monopolistic public utility holding companies. There were other significant laws that added up to the inauguration of a welfare state, replacing the libertarian state. Truman supported these great domestic initiatives. On the foreign policy front, war in Asia, Africa, and Europe had to be dealt with. American isolationism and noninterventionism led to passage of the Neutrality Acts of 1935, 1936, and 1937, which Truman supported. For now, Truman was a "go along to get along" supporter of New Deal legislation, while being personally sour on the president and his inner circle, a duality that gave him the reputation of a maverick. Later, his disagreement on some bills strengthened this image.

Truman's mindset in the summer of 1935 was set forth in a letter to Bess: "I am hoping to make a reputation as a Senator, though if I live long enough that'll make the money successes look like cheese. But you will have to put up with a lot if I do it because I won't sell influence and I'm perfectly willing to be cussed if I'm right." He tried to remain upright and not trade favors. Then he played into his double self as he traveled to New York City to see Pendergast, who was visiting like a prince at the Waldorf Astoria, the same place where millionaire Joseph P. Kennedy had his office. Apparently, both princes could afford such accommodations. All we know is that Truman and Pendergast talked local, and not national, politics.

Truman spent the previous summer of 1935 alone and desolate. He had paired on an important farm bill—that is, his yea vote was matched with a nay vote—in order to be free to drive Bess and Margaret home to Independence. He then returned alone to Washington. His letters to Bess, after his return, are heartbreaking. On the 17th of June: "I miss you terribly"; on the 18th: "I've been walking around like a lost soul this morning. . . . It's a wrench to be without you. I never missed you so much before"; on the 28th: "You have been married to a financial failure." Presumably, if he had money, they could have a house and live in Washington all year round. So, Truman scrimped where he could; he rode the bus to the Senate and garaged the car as too expensive to run, and he ate at Childs Restaurant, noted for its indifferent food. In his letters to Bess in July (the 9th and 11th) he suggested that they rent an apartment or house on a year's lease.

On July 23 he exploded: "We'll never do this again. We've got to work out some way to make ends meet and have a place to live in Washington." Bess must have replied negatively, and he wrote on the 29th: "I am disappointed that you didn't look with favor on coming back." Truman, staying at the Continental Hotel, complained of a "terrific headache" on December 6, but thought he only needed new glasses. On the 8th, he wrote Bess of "torment." A headache came on, again, on January 3, 1936, and he wanted to get a house in Washington, as he had received his World War I bonus, probably the maximum of $500, about $5,000 in today's dollars. On January 5, Truman wrote to Bess: "I just can't stand it without you. If we were poorer than church mice, what difference does it make? There is only one thing that counts with me and that is you and Margie." He mentioned an invitation to Bess from Mrs. Roosevelt for January 13. "You are supposed to be there. . . . I *want you to be present*." But Bess stayed home. She loved her husband but must have hated their cramped, small apartments—a different one each year—as compared to her mother's commodious house in Independence. And Margaret went to schools for one term in each city, to private Gunston Hall when in Washington, and to the public school in Independence. It seemed, to Bess at least, a good plan. And Bess was her mother's sole housekeeper and aide.

To Bess, Truman complained of eye trouble, sick spells, headaches, and tiredness. He reported a mild inflammation of the heart muscle and mild edema. The cause, he was told, was nervous strain and overwork. The principal difficulty, doctors concluded, was starvation. The lonely bachelor was not taking care of himself, even his minimal need to eat.

In 1936, Truman went to the Democratic National Convention in Philadelphia and was seen in the friendly company of Pendergast. All the machine bosses were there, as the party had become a congeries of interests that was made of cities, labor, and the South. Immense amounts of money from New Deal programs kept the coalition strong. Pendergast was of necessity a presence in Truman's senatorial life because of the Boss's command of patronage, small but on a broad scale, involving postmasterships and WPA jobs. The scramble for the former had not changed since Andrew Jackson's time, and only civil service reform after the Civil War had changed things a bit with exams required. Still, postmasterships were good jobs in a depression. The salaries were small, but the job had few duties. WPA jobs, however, were better, if not as secure. Seventy-four million dollars of WPA money were poured into Missouri. The agency and Pendergast were joined at the hip.

Along with Truman's senatorial and health troubles, he got the bad news that his mother's farm was going to be seized by the bank on December 1, 1937, for mortgage and taxes. Truman seemed to be ailing a good deal at this time, with some body responses triggered by psychosomatic causes. The body didn't care that the traumas were new. Its response was now a learned one.

Truman's hard work—he studied every bill carefully and ordered dozens of books from the Library of Congress to learn about legislation—was beginning to bear fruit and show promise. He chaired a subcommittee on railroads that was holding hearings on a plan to reorganize the nation's railroads. He found the roads hellishly mismanaged; stocks were watered and sold to investors, and the roads were deteriorating for lack of repair. Scandalous malfeasance in the country's railroads was not a new story, and now it was happening again. Farmers and industry now depended on railroads, as waterways and canals had become secondary carriers. Progress depended on railroads. While

Truman was careful to protect Missouri's railroads, he charged others with "immoral and illegal behavior." In a speech in June 1937, he declared that the roads had been looted and that those in charge were "vultures at the death of an elephant." He suggested having the holding companies involved dissolved.

Truman was sounding like trust-busting Teddy Roosevelt, but his mentor was Louis Brandeis. The great Progressive lawyer from Massachusetts asked to meet the junior senator from Missouri and invited him to tea at his house. Brandeis had cleaned up industries, such as insurance, that were fleecing people. He pioneered what were later dubbed Brandeis Briefs, which were fact-laden and well-argued. He was also known for his hostility to bigness. He took down companies in Massachusetts for illegal and unethical practices. In 1916, Woodrow Wilson had appointed Brandeis to the Supreme Court, where he became one of the most admired justices in its history, serving until 1939. Truman seemed bitten by Brandeis, and gave a second speech in December on large insurance companies, holding companies, and concentrations of wealth that was almost pure Brandeis:

> We worship Mammon; and until we go back to fundamentals and return to the Giver of the Tables of Law and His teachings, these conditions are going to remain with us.... I believe the country would be better off if we did not have sixty percent of the assets of all the insurance companies concentrated in four companies. I believe that a thousand insurance companies, with $4,000,000 each in assets, would be just a thousand times better for the country than the Metropolitan Life,

with $4,000,000,000 in assets. . . . Our unemployment and our unrest are the result of the concentration of wealth, the concentration of population in industrial centers, mass production, and a lot of other so-called modern improvements.

Truman's hearings on the railroads went on for months and resulted in four bills, forming an ambitious program. The full Senate cobbled together a single bill and sent it to the House and a conference committee. A bill returned to the House, where it was defeated. Few were ready for a grand reorganization of the railroads, the first ever tried even after countless scandals about these iron horses over the decades. In 1940, a Transportation Act was finally passed, but it was little help to the still struggling railroads. One historian called it a "quaint, nostalgic, even reactionary" act. Truman's bitter words were: "I feel like four years and a half's work has been thrown into the river."

The railroad fiasco was a tough learning experience for Truman: how hearings were conducted, how bills were subjected to varying and contending interests, and how a final act could accomplish little, after months or even years of work. His one win was saving the Missouri Railroad from bankruptcy. He was still a home boy. Besides, the save meant a leg up the next time he ran for the Senate. It was a necessary, if not virtuous, act for him.

Truman's voting record remained spotty on the New Deal coalition. For example, Senator Alben Barkley of Kentucky was one of the ornaments of the Roosevelt administration, but when Truman was asked to support him for Senate majority leader, he refused. Barkley and Truman were not friends at this time, but ironically, the Kentuckian would play a prominent role in the Truman presidency. Working with the New Deal coalition, Truman opposed cutting appropriations for relief payments. He tried to protect the little guy who could not find a job to support his family. And when FDR tried to add six new justices to the Supreme Court, to combat those who were striking down his New Deal programs, the senator supported his president. Truman also favored the Roosevelt bill to reorganize the executive branch of government. But he became known for his open, cutting quips about the New Deal because he was uneasy about the growth of the government and its reorganization of the economy. His instincts were less Hamiltonian—strong central government—than were those of New Dealers, and he slid around in Jeffersonian and Bryanesque bogs, that is, protecting farmers and laborers. His strongest instincts were to help the little toilers and not the big capitalists. After all, he was one of them, although he had tried so many ill-fated times to become rich. He knew how difficult it was to rise in the nation and how many roadblocks were put up by corporations and rich people to that desire.

So far, Truman could claim no legislative achievements. Worse, he held too tightly to his roots back home, even though the Pendergast machine was being legally pummeled, and a new Democratic governor, Lloyd Stark, was cleaning up corruption and proving to be a progressive leader. By the end of 1938, the toll was 278 indictments, 63 convictions, 196 pleas of guilty or no-contest, 72 prison sentences, and over $60,000 in fines. Truman could have turned his back on his old pals at this point, as did other political leaders in other states when their corrupt machines were exposed, but he did not. From his army days onward, he put loyalty above all other virtues. In fact, he voted against the reappointment of the crusading US attorney general, who was upending the Pendergast machine. On the Senate floor, he actually attacked the attorney general and his aides. He ranted that "a Jackson County, Missouri, Democrat has as much chance of a fair trial in the Federal District Court of Western Missouri as a Jew would have in a Hitler court or a Trotsky follower before Stalin. Indictments have been wholesale. Convictions have been a foregone conclusion. Verdicts have been directed. This is Federal court justice in Western Missouri, on the face of it a conspiracy between the partisan Federal judges and their bought and paid for district attorney."

The local newspaper attacked Truman for his moralizing and tactics. The *New York Times* wrote: "Say *not* the struggle naught availeth. Tom Pendergast may have lost the cemetery vote, but he can't lose Harry Truman." What was in Truman's tortured, divided self was embarrassing at the time and is still not understood today. The underlying psychological source is revelatory only in a careful and nuanced reading of the Pickwick Papers.

There was a seesaw battle in Kansas City between Pendergast and the anti-corruption forces. The Boss could still win a municipal election, although the voting lists had been cleaned up, but the Justice Department, with the Treasury Department, had targeted his machine. One hundred sixty-seven indictments came down in mid-March 1938, and then a federal grand jury indicted Pendergast for tax fraud. Once more Truman chose to step into the mud puddle to declare publicly that "political animus" was behind the indictment. "I'm sorry it happened. My connection with Pendergast was, of course, purely political. He has been a friend to me when I needed it. I am not one to desert a ship when it starts to go down." How could such a statement possibly have helped his reputation? What was he thinking? Then there were resignations back home of politicos, and the Boss went to prison.

Truman reflected that all this legal action against corruption vindicated his own honesty. That fall he wrote Bess: "Looks like everybody in Jackson County got rich but me. I'm glad I can sleep well even if it is a hardship on you and Margie for me to be so damn poor." We don't know how Bess felt about their "poverty," but she must have known that her husband was the last man standing in the Pendergast playground. When the reformers planned to run the newly famous governor, Stark, for senator against Truman, her husband replied: "I'll beat the hell out of him." Then Vivian lost his patronage job via the Truman adversaries. It seemed the last straw. Truman thought of resigning. But only for a moment. He would leave town and the poisonous atmosphere and take a tour of army bases in the United States, Central America, Panama, and then back up the West Coast. As he put it, he "decided to run away from it for a while." His divided self fell into the old pattern of how to deal with political trouble. But now, he left no secret written record of his anguish, no Pickwick Papers.

Reality came to the fore, as Truman had to decide on a second term. Being a senator was the only way he knew to support his family. He would run again. He knew he was not a professional man, a lawyer, an accountant, a man with business connections, who could make a living out of the public sphere, so up against the wall, he looked over the political landscape back home. He would be headed for a vicious campaign. Jim Pendergast would help. The Masons, who had given him small sums for speeches, would assist. Army buddies would rally. He saw that he was weak in St. Louis and northwestern Missouri. The southwestern part of the state was dicey, and central Missouri would help him, as Bennett Clark was now on his side, a positive, and WPA jobs were plentiful through what remained of the Pendergast machine. These men would rally to him. Kansas City seemed indifferent. The *Post-Dispatch* wrote on January 6, 1940: "He is a dead cock in the pit."

Truman filed for renomination the next month, more as an act of defiance of the fates than with a hope for winning. He had never been personally accused of fraud or corruption, and that would help. That his own mother was bankrupt, as heartbreaking as that was, showed he was a poor man, hardly on the take. The grateful railroad brotherhood of 50,000 men supported him. The American Federation of Labor was on his side. A few key senators were keen on him. Jimmy Byrnes got $4,000 from millionaire Bernard Baruch to help Truman. The war in Europe, although not high on Missourians' radar screen, assisted Truman, who was a veteran and defense expert—he was on the military appropriations subcommittee and had recently toured bases. The newspapers, however, were another kettle of fish. The *Star Times, Post-Dispatch,* and *Globe-Democrat* opposed him. Only the *Kansas City Journal* was in his corner. The editors of the *Post-Dispatch,* always able to write with verve, commented: "Should Truman be nominated, there would be shrill rejoicing among all the forces of evil in Missouri." It was the paper of rectitude and social conscience, run by the old elite, and reformist. Truman did not pass the smell test because of his long, and never severed, connection, with the Pendergast machine. Then, surprisingly, blunders by Governor Stark jolted the campaign. For example, he ignored black voters and the remnants of the Pendergast machine. On the question of blacks, Truman was about where Lincoln was before the Civil War. The senator believed not in social equality for blacks but in equality of opportunity. And he stressed "the brotherhood of all men before the law." Blacks were a respected interest group in his campaign. He had supported legislation to abolish the poll tax and to end lynchings. He had also voted to end the filibuster against the anti-lynching bill. He was in the vanguard, but the Senate was, basically, right of center on social issues. And the South, with its racist, often vicious views, was a fundamental and large part of the Democratic Party, which the political leaders did not want to alienate.

The byzantine politics in Missouri helped Truman, as his strong opponent, Stark, continued to make mistakes by alienating parts of the Democratic coalition. Stark lost control of the state's delegation to the 1940 Democratic National Convention, where the party supported Roosevelt for a third term. But

Stark's decline did not automatically raise Truman. Would the cool Roosevelt intervene to help or hurt Truman? The president had never warmed to Truman, and now Truman did not help his reelection cause when he said he opposed third terms for presidents in principle but was waiving this principle for Roosevelt. Truman had seemed a good New Dealer in so many of his Senate votes. But he had strayed at awkward times, as when he voted to deny an administration proposal to bring the Civil Aeronautics Authority under the Commerce Department, and, when Roosevelt vetoed Truman's bill to give government funds for railroad bridges, Truman led the Senate in an override. He was in and out of the New Deal. Roosevelt was keeping his ace in the hole regarding Missouri politics.

Mid-June 1940 found Truman in his formal campaign mode, even putting his eighty-seven-year-old mother next to him at political events (early shades of when John F. Kennedy did the same thing in 1960). Truman gave a stump speech across the state. Its basic elements were that he favored a strong national defense, a break for blacks, and equity for farmers. Governor Stark, who was considered the strongest candidate, was running on a platform that stressed his moral rectitude. But he was now revealed to be involved in schemes for kickbacks and taking money from lobbyists. Then Truman got help from the senior senator, Bennett Clark, in a speech that made fun of the famously super-ambitious governor, trying to kill him with comedy. Bennett accused Stark of "simultaneously running for president, vice president, secretary of war, secretary of the navy, high commissioner of the Philippines, ambassador to Great

Britain, and United States Senator. It was also rumored . . . that he is a receptive candidate for the papacy and the archbishopric of Canterbury." Clark tickled audiences, long used to dull campaign speeches. When Stark tried his wings against Henry Wallace, Roosevelt's candidate for the vice presidency, the game was up. Clark turned on Stark, calling this attempt "ill-fated, short-lived, and a ludicrous fiasco."

Truman was now an old hand at campaigning. He got into his car and re-mapped his 1934 trail. He took along a basic speech but added flourishes for different audiences: labor, farmers, veterans. He visited seventy-five counties during the hot July of 1940. He did not look upon his term in office as anything near a failure, or even a disappointment, and was received politely. Unions gave his campaign money, and, once more, Baruch helped with funds. Still, Truman was short of money, and it was reported that he inquired about a loan against his life insurance.

The battle for the nomination was as dirty as Missouri politics usually got. The uncharismatic Truman's audiences were sparse. The *Post-Dispatch* charged—falsely—that Truman supporters were trying to demand money from WPA workers in exchange for keeping their jobs. The *Kansas City Star* ran an old picture of Truman under a Pendergast portrait. Truman went to bed thinking he had lost the primary election. It would not be the last time he would do this, for we recall 1948, when no one, no influentials, thought he could win. But St. Louis came through for him, as did Jackson County. He carried five more counties than he did in 1934, forty-four in all. Stark charged that Truman had stolen the election with Pendergast votes in the big cities and the southeast. Maybe. Truman, in turn, was bitter about Stark. On Truman's return to Washington, a supporter of the governor asked if the senator had heard from Stark about losing the primary. In a letter to Bess, Truman relates his reply: "I hadn't and didn't want to hear from the S.O.B. and that so far as I am concerned I didn't give a damn what he did or intended to do, and that I hoped he'd tell him just that." Truman savored his primary victory. He told Bess on August 9, "I'll never forget Tuesday night if I live to be a thousand." The next day, he wrote that when he slipped back into the Senate, there was a rush toward him. "I thought Wheeler and Jim Byrnes were going to kiss me. Barkley and Harrison were almost as effusive. Schwellenbach, Hatch, Lister Hill, and Tom Stewart almost beat me to death. . . . [Sherman] Minton hugged me."

His euphoria was lessened when his mother finally had to move from the farm the family had lived in since 1868. The bank made a profit of $1,600, and Truman suggested that Mamma and Mary Jane rent a house in Grandview. Then Truman reported to Bess how things were going in late August, on the 27th. He voted for the Selective Service and Training Act, a big appropriations bill, and the Transportation Act, and he awaited an upcoming new tax bill.

In the general election, Truman was, once more, hammered about his Pendergast background. He persevered and campaigned over the whole state. He won with 51.2 percent of the vote, as Roosevelt won by 52.3 percent. It would be hard to say who had the coattails. Truman won, thanks to the cities' vote. The pattern, overall, was similar to his 1934 victory and that of New Dealers in the nation in 1940. He has always been portrayed as a staunch New Dealer as a senator, but that picture needs retouching. Never fully accepted by Roosevelt until 1940, when the president needed him, Truman had been more of a country than a city politician, until now. Farmers were central to his success. Now laboring groups in cities supported him, too. On some issues, such as civil rights, he was more cautious than the national party, and he was more tied to machine politics than many other politicians who had begun shunning such corrupt connections. Truman wiggled as a maverick. He was no Senator Robert Wagner of New York, a prime architect of the New Deal.

Truman left Missouri politics now to the boys back home. He had had enough of its scandal, disloyalty, and betrayal. He decided that Washington was going to be his political home. National politics was to be his métier. He would have six more years to show his stuff. He might retire, again he noted, after that. He had learned some good lessons about committee work, even though the Senate and House made shambles of many bills he felt strongly about. He had watched how interest-group politics worked, and he noticed how disconnected morality could be from practical politics. Getting things done was the supreme aim in politics. He reminisced in his *Autobiography*— which is not always accurate—that only once did Pendergast ask him for a favor: to vote for Alben Barkley for majority leader in the Senate. He didn't, and suffered no consequences.

It was refreshing. Truman was now going to try to be his own man.

When Truman's second term began, the world was on fire. Alone, England was holding out against Hitler's onslaught and was desperately in need of aid. Belgium, the Netherlands, Norway, and even the supposedly impregnable France—after all, it had built the Maginot Line against Germany—had all been conquered. Roosevelt's solution was to send arms to England on credit. But it stirred up midwestern senators, who had been isolationists from years ago. Some of Truman's friends opposed the aid. Senator Wheeler was the most outrageous in his use of language, claiming a war would "plow under every fourth American boy." Clark, the senior senator from Missouri, opposed Lend-Lease, the administration program that allowed Allies to get war equipment, with the costs to be repaid later. But Truman, the brave captain and veteran, supported Roosevelt against a number of crippling amendments proposed to negate the bill. He also voted for the Selective Service and Training Act and even tried to enlist, as had Theodore Roosevelt when America entered World War I. Like TR, he was turned down, but for his age and not for a method of fighting Roosevelt had proposed to President Wilson, who did not need Rough Riders in this war, a modern conflict of machine guns, tanks, and airplanes, unlike that of 1898.

It took an impending war to get Bess to stay in Washington the whole year. Truman was allowed five assistants, and Bess was one. She showed up for work every day. Her annual salary was now raised to $4,500. Her mother, living with the Trumans in Washington, slept in a twin bed in Margaret's room. The Trumans' actual, not relative, poverty was noticeable.

In mail and phone calls, Truman was beginning to hear about military mismanagement in his own backyard regarding what all suspected was a coming war. Construction at Fort Leonard Wood in Missouri was slipshod, and contracts were going out of state. Perhaps the latter troubled Missourians more than the former, the Depression still ongoing, but Truman was more interested in malfeasance. He got into his car and drove 10,000 miles, on his own nickel, inspecting camps and construction, and was horrified by what he witnessed. Big companies were making excessive profits for shoddy work, and the cost-plus arrangement—a fixed cost plus a profit—used by the army was leading to corruption. He asked to see the president and was flabbergasted by a cordial welcome. Undoubtedly, Harry told him what he found out and that he was preparing a speech on the subject in the Senate.

On February 10, 1941, Truman laid it all out before the Senate and asked for the establishment of a special committee to oversee defense contracts. In December, $10 billion had been voted for defense, an immense amount of money. Another billion had also been requested and a two-million-man army was to be called up. Truman knew from his own military experiences how such large amounts of money would attract dishonesty. Beyond this worry, Truman also was not happy that military contracts were being awarded by the War Department without listening to congressmen's suggestions. It was de rigueur that congressmen were listened to. They wanted the

FIGURE 13   Harry S. Truman in 1942 at a session of the United States Senate's Special Committee to Investigate the National Defense Program, of which he was chairman. Pictured from left to right at the counsel table are Senator James M. Mead, Democrat from New York; Charles Patrick Clark, associate chief counsel; Senator Truman; and Senator Owen Brewster, Republican of Maine. *Credit:* Office of War Information, courtesy of the Harry S. Truman Library.

defense money spread around to give jobs in the bad economy. The administration was cool to Truman's notion of oversight— so much for his cordial presidential visit—because it wanted no meddling. The War Department agreed and added that such a system would slow up rearmament. Only General George Marshall—that soon-to-be paragon of military service to his country—favored Truman's plans, and surprisingly, Roosevelt changed his mind. He was persuaded that, in friendly hands, that is, Truman's, the investigations could go well. In a show of how the Senate looked down on all this—maybe it recalled how baneful such a committee had been during the Civil War—it gave Truman a paltry $15,000 in March to investigate. Later, he

got an additional $50,000, but only after he began issuing re-
markable reports about fraud and corruption that were hurting
the defense effort. At the same time, Congress voted $7 billion
for Lend-Lease. Truman took on the staggering task of making
war contracts honest, with little money for investigators, against
a mountain of cash backing crooked contractors. But, so successful was his work that the committee ultimately got a million
dollars to continue its investigations.

The name of Truman's committee, the Special Committee
to Investigate the National Defense Program, describes its purpose well. The committee had, as its aim, the gathering of information on the monetary and actual performance of thirty
national programs intended to build military camps, airplane
engines, steel plates, maintenance contracts, and sundry other
contracts intended to win a war. Harry wrote to Bess on March
19, 1941: "My investigating committee is getting really hot. Feel
better about it now. Looks like I'll get something done." In a letter on June 19 he wrote that, as a result of his investigation, his
"standing in the Senate and down the street [the White House]
gets better and better."

The committee had five Democrats and two Republicans on
it, assuring that it would not embarrass the administration. Truman chose the members, except for the Texan Tom Connally,
whose goal was to run interference for the president. The committee had more than eighteen clerks, investigators, and lawyers.
Its highly regarded chief counsel Hugh Fulton ran a model investigation, although Truman was the chief interrogator, percep-
tive and strong, but never harsh. Top members met frequently

in Truman's office—"Harry's Doghouse," as they called it—to discuss findings and plans. Truman said his aim was just to help the president. Early on, he attacked waste and fraud. He gave the Senate annual reports, sitting as chairman until 1944, although the committee worked until 1948. The committee's Truman years were considered a great success. The committee's work on mobilization was essential, so slack was the bureaucracy. Even though it was not tasked to influence policy, it did.

Over its lifespan to 1948, the committee issued fifty-one reports totaling 1,946 pages. It held 432 public hearings at which 1,798 witnesses made 2,284 appearances, producing forty-three volumes of printed testimony, totaling 27,568 pages. It held 300 private meetings, taking 25,000 additional pages of transcript. That was the end product. It was a staggering achievement.

Before we detail some important aspects of the committee's work, a personal note is needed. The burdens of the special committee and his other committee assignments were affecting Truman's health. He checked into a hospital for a week in July 1941. Truman gave Bess full rundowns of visits of doctors in a series of letters. On July 5 he reported that "fatigue" was his problem. It was also a time when both his mother and brother-in-law Fred seemed to be ailing. Then, Madge Gates, his mother-in-law, was ill, but also doing better, he was told. On July 7, Truman had "spasms." Probably worried, Bess went to see Harry in Washington in August but didn't stay long. The psychological strain and the psychosomatic aspects of his ailments can be seen in a letter he wrote from Hot Springs, Virginia, on May 1, 1942, which includes this plaintive revelation:

"Mommy, I've wanted so badly to make good in the Senate so you and my sweet baby won't be ashamed of me."

Truman rallied and went about investigating camps, construction, and plane manufacturing. He kept Bess apprised as he visited Knoxville, Memphis, Dallas, San Diego, San Francisco, Seattle, Chicago, and in his home state, St. Louis, Springfield, and Carruthersville. He told Bess: "Labor is a problem. The same brand of racketeer is getting his hand in as he did in the camp construction program. Some of them should be in jail." So, in an irony of fate, Truman's Pendergast years gave him insight and moxie to uncover fraud and corruption that curtailed progress. He pointed out that he especially disliked the "cutthroat monopoly" of aluminum companies, which were making airplanes. He favored using magnesium, a cheaper metal, to make planes, but he was in fact wrong in preferring this weaker metal.

The roving senator always felt better away from Washington, "both mentally and physically," he recorded. But when he went back home he was pulled into home politics. He met with Jim Pendergast and others to discuss Kansas City politics. He was also brought up to date on other local and state affairs. He found out that the senior senator was not taking care of business and was drinking too much. He was implored to save the party that had given him so much trouble in his primary, when newcomers were allowed too much power. He wasn't interested in protecting the depleted Pendergast wing.

On the way back to Washington, Truman stopped at Appomattox and reflected on Robert E. Lee, one of his heroes. He thought of what Lee must have endured in the days before he surrendered. He ruminated to Bess and said that a great man can take defeat and still be great. Lee was one and, maybe, Lincoln. Lee was Truman's great war hero, a superb general and moral man. Second was Washington. Truman continued: "We are in the midst of one of the periods of history—and that is what sometimes gives your old man the headache and the pain in the middle. . . . What we do is of vital importance to our daughter's generation and the next one." This was November 1941. He then told Bess—we don't know why, at this time— how he had almost passed out when Henry Wallace was nominated for vice president in 1940. Wallace, a distinguished geneticist, agrarian, and politician from Iowa, was too mystical for Truman, who had become a hard-boiled politician by this point. Roosevelt easily won reelection against the novice Republican Wendell Willkie. And Congress remained Democratic. The main issue was the war, and Roosevelt promised that he would not take the country into a foreign war. Truman reported continuing stress to his system at the time, and he saw no easy way out.

And then the war came on December 7, 1941. Truman rushed back to Washington to hear Roosevelt address Congress. "A date that will live in infamy" was the headline of the historic address about Japan's sneak attack on Pearl Harbor that crippled America's world-class navy. Truman had planned to go home for Christmas but to brief Roosevelt on his committee's work before he left. He was furious that the president waited until Truman had gone home and then called him back. Truman had to break off his vacation to return to Washington. He wrote to Bess: "It must be done or I'd tell him to go to hell. He's so damned afraid that he won't have all the power and glory that he won't let his friends help as it should be done." It is one of the tragedies of history that Roosevelt and Truman never became friends and shared confidences. The two men, from different classes and political origins, were fated to be unknown to each other, to the nation's loss.

How has the committee been received in history? Some of Truman's accomplishments involved clawbacks of excessive profits from contractors. Perhaps a quarter of these before-taxes profits were returned. Estimates are that $15 billion were saved, more than $150 billion in today's dollars. James Forrestal, representing the War Department, thought the committee's work was "constructive." Robert P. Patterson, representing the army and air force, was not cooperative. The committee probably adopted Truman's own jaundiced view of the professional military from his war years. His work, however, seemed to win Americans' approval, and his seeing that contracts were spread around the country was applauded. He became a household name. Truman ran a responsible, restrained committee, getting in no one's way in the Congress or administration. Its admirable reputation remains in history. In 2008, in an August 6 article in the *Wall Street Journal*, New York Senator Hillary Clinton wrote, "In the Democratic Congress, we've proposed a new Truman Committee to address the waste, fraud and abuse in Iraq and Afghanistan. . . . Of course we need far more than a Truman Committee. . . . We need the Truman spirit in the White House, where the buck finally stops." Her proposal was buried by the Bush White House and on Republican orders.

Truman's main work during the war, which raged on, was with the special committee. His contribution to the war's success was becoming well known, and its probity polished his reputation, which began so tarnished in 1935. He followed the war's progress, both in Europe and Asia, and his own war experience gave him good insights into how the war was being conducted. He had always been on the Allied side, favored giving England old submarines in Lend-Lease laws as well as monies sorely needed, as the war was bankrupting England, that once reigning nation in the world. And he knew any postwar world would diminish England's role in world events—it would be America's Century. The burden on the United States would be tremendous. He favored a United Nations organization to try to preserve the peace in the future. His hatred of Hitler, Japan, and their deeds was immense, and he knew the war would be long and brutal.

In 1944, when Roosevelt decided to run for a fourth term, the big question was with whom would he partner? All the war horses had negatives except, it seemed, Harry Truman. He was the man in the spotlight saving the country vast amounts of money and actually directing some defense decisions because his investigations uncovered alternatives to some weapons programs. But vice president? Getting to his candidacy would prove to be a crooked path, full of deception on Roosevelt's part and byzantine politics within the party. Early in the summer of 1943, Truman had a feeler from a New Deal senator, and Truman responded that he was not interested. Truman based this on his belief that Roosevelt did not like him. Two horses pulling a chariot in different directions would not win a race. Then Wallace, the present vice president, wanted to run again. Some Roosevelt insiders thought he had made a splendid Secretary of Agriculture but was now "too intellectual, a mystic who spoke Russian, played with a boomerang, and reputedly consulted with the spirit of a dead Sioux Indian Chief." What a mix of charges!

Jimmy Byrnes thought Roosevelt was bowing in his direction, but he had left his Catholic faith, and the party was very Catholic, especially in many big cities. Labor was cool to him and, because he was from South Carolina, some considered him a racist; after all, he had opposed the anti-lynching law in 1938. Senator Barkley, a popular and likable senator, was held in reserve. Truman continued to say no, when asked, because he thought the job boring—was it true, as John Nance Garner had said, that it was not worth a bucket of warm spit? And Bess was opposed to Harry's being elevated. Truman wrote to Margaret: "1600 Pennsylvania Avenue is a nice address but I'd rather not move through the back door—or any other door at sixty." That was an odd statement, unless Truman felt Roosevelt would die soon, based on his own observation of the president's faltering, if not failing, health. Roosevelt played his games, encouraging Byrnes and Wallace, while his advisers told him that Truman would lose him the fewest votes in the election. It was a backhanded compliment. Truman acceded to Byrnes's request to nominate him at the convention, assuring him that he himself was not a candidate for the office. Barkley then called Truman but learned that he was already taken for the nomination job.

What had made Truman the dark horse candidate in the bitter race for vice president? The committee work kept him healthy, and there were no more letters to Bess mentioning nausea, headaches, and the fear of a heart attack. He dressed nattily and wore his World War I pin on his lapel. His demeanor in running his committee was courteous and affable, while he asked probing questions. He had been put on the cover of *Time* magazine on March 8, 1943, and the influential Arthur Krock, the Washington bureau chief of the *New York Times,* wrote that Truman made "an excellent impression."

Truman's family life was quiet, tied up in a loving knot. He made time, finally, to speak out about war aims, foreseeing the United States as the world's next leader—move over England, the great imperial power for a hundred years—and supported a United Nations, a great cause of First Lady Eleanor Roosevelt, who would become the first US delegate to the body. Of the many successes of his committee, and often overlooked, is its sponsorship and support of the Higgins landing craft, which could land troops, quickly, anywhere, on shallow beaches, instead of in known harbors, subject to attack. Historians give the boats enormous credit for the success of the Normandy landings in 1944.

In his investigations, Truman got wind of what later became known as the Manhattan Project to build an atomic bomb, because of the immense amounts of money hidden in accounts. Secretary of War Stimson told him, over the phone, that the ap-

propriation was for "a very important secret development." It
was for "a unique purpose." The subject was dropped. Truman
was later indiscreet when he wrote to a former senator and
friend that a plant was being built to make "a terrific explosion
for a secret weapon that will be a wonder." When a senator
asked for information in November 1944 about the subject, the
War Department was contacted, again, and it told Truman that
no more information about the project would be forthcoming.
Truman backed off. Then he poked into the secret once more.
Stimson found Truman "a nuisance and a pretty untrustworthy
man." The secretary had become high-handed by this time in
his career. A longtime government official, whose career had
begun under Theodore Roosevelt, of an elite background in
every way, he was not used to being questioned, once he had
made a decision on whom to include and exclude regarding
government secrets. He ordered: "Under no circumstances is
Senator Truman to be told anything more." In early 1945 Sam
Rayburn, the Speaker of the House, and John McCormack and
Joseph Martin, majority and minority leaders, were fully briefed
about the atomic bomb by Stimson, General Marshall, and Vannevar Bush, head of the Office of Scientific Research. It wasn't
until Truman became the accidental president in April 1945
that he learned of the atomic bomb.

Meanwhile, as the choice for vice president was being made,
Eleanor Roosevelt, who never stopped being active in Democratic politics, wrote to Henry Wallace that Truman was a good
man. The senator seemed to have no enemies in Washington.
President Roosevelt continued his game of cat and mouse on

the vice presidency, and had a seizure on the very day of his nomination. Only his son, Jimmy, now a constant companion, was a witness. It was not known at the time, even in the closest circles, that Roosevelt was ill with congestive heart failure, but newly discovered records from the Lahey Clinic outside Boston confirm it.

Twists and turns abounded, as Roosevelt and his advisers before, and at the beginning, of the Democratic convention, officially opening on July 19, could not all agree on the right vice presidential candidate. Truman told a reporter: "Hell, I don't want to be president," when he learned that too many of the journalists assumed that the vice president would be the next president. He meant it. Ed Flynn, the powerful New York boss, took charge when he arrived at the convention and saw the party being whipsawed among candidates, with Roosevelt playing the devil (it seemed). FDR was for and against all the candidates being bandied about. He always loved toying with the men around him. So Flynn called Roosevelt, who agreed on Truman. Truman called and told Byrnes, whose calls were then not taken by Roosevelt as a waste of his time. FDR may have felt a bit of guilt over not choosing his once-close associate for the job. Byrnes dropped out. Truman confided to his friend Charlie Ross: "Feel sorry for me. I'm in a terrible fix." He was called to a meeting of the president's inner circle and Roosevelt checked in by phone to see whether they had persuaded Truman to run with him. It was determined that the president had to talk to Truman himself, and he said to Truman that if he did not run he would split the party during a war. Did he want this?

FIGURE 14 Vice-presidential candidate Harry S. Truman at lunch with President Franklin D. Roosevelt on the White House lawn, August 21, 1944. *Credit:* Office of War Information, courtesy of the Harry S. Truman Library.

Truman blurted out: "Oh, shit." Then, "Well, if that's the situation, I'll have to say yes." He then added, "but why the hell didn't he tell me in the first place?" Roosevelt must have used such strong language because Wallace was very popular, but he held political views counter to Roosevelt's. The president could not allow such a difference: the vice president had to be in sync with the president. The convention could not give Truman the victory on the first ballot, however, as Wallace would not give up. A plan was concocted to put up sixteen names to block him. Still Wallace was leading at the end of the first ballot. Truman prevailed on the second ballot with 1,031 votes, Wallace 105, Supreme Court Associate Justice William O. Douglas 4. Bess gave up her grumpy face and smiled, while Margaret, elated, jumped up and down. Truman gave a short acceptance speech and ended with: "Now give me a chance."

Roosevelt and Truman had lunch on August 21. Truman looked robust, the president haggard. And the president's "hands were shaking and he talks with considerable difficulty.... It doesn't seem to be any mental lapse of any kind but physically he's just going to pieces," Truman told a friend. The friend said that he might be soon in the White House. Harry retorted: "It scares the hell out of me."

The campaign against Truman was dirty, but that was nothing new. Everyone knew of his political origins, but no one knew of Bess's father's suicide, her deepest secret, which kept her cool, always cool, toward public life. Except for calling her "Payroll Bess," the campaign was really against Roosevelt. The election was the closest since 1916, when Wilson pulled off a victory for keeping the United States out of the raging First World War. Roosevelt held a 3 million vote margin, and it gave him thirty-six states. The inauguration was simple and short, reminiscent of Lincoln's, who was an earlier wartime president beset with a world of troubles.

Vice President Truman experienced the normal career in that office for eighty-two days. He mostly presided over the Senate, as was his constitutional duty. With no committees, he was like a bystander at a wedding. Roosevelt slipped away to Yalta, to meet with Churchill and Stalin to reorganize Europe after the war, without telling the vice president. Truman had no contact with the president or with Secretary of State Edward Stettinius, another member of the nation's ruling elite. The

FIGURE 15 Actress Lauren Bacall sits atop a piano while Vice President Harry Truman plays at the National Press Club Canteen, February 10, 1945. They were at the canteen to entertain the servicemen. *Credit:* Harris & Ewing, courtesy of the Harry S. Truman Library.

Trumans and Madge Wallace stayed in their five-room apartment. The only perk the vice president received was a limousine and driver. He was seen playing the piano, with the gorgeous movie star Lauren Bacall draped over it and Harry grinning like the Cheshire cat. Bess was as furious as the press was delighted.

On his return from abroad, on March 1, 1945, a weary Franklin Roosevelt addressed the Congress. "I hope that you will pardon me for this unusual posture of sitting down during the presentation of what I want to say," he began, "but I know that you will realize that it makes it a lot easier for me not to have to carry about ten pounds of steel around on the bottom of my legs; and also because of the fact that I have just completed a fourteen-thousand-mile trip." Germany was near collapse, the president said. He envisioned the beginnings of a postwar world, including the founding of the United Nations. Truman had seen the president only two times since his victory and knew nothing of the affairs of the White House. On April 12, 1945, Truman was at a social gathering—Sam Rayburn's Board of Education. A call came to Truman from the White House, and he was to call back right away. Truman mixed himself a drink—bourbon—and dialed National 1414. He was told to come to the White House, "as quickly and as quietly" as he could, to the main entrance on Pennsylvania Avenue. "Jesus Christ and General Jackson," Truman blurted out. He retrieved his hat and ran to his limousine. He arrived at 5:25. Mrs. Roosevelt met him in the private quarters upstairs, and gently touching his shoulder, said, "Harry, the president is dead."

"Is there anything I can do for you?" he replied.

The famously gracious First Lady responded, "Is there anything *we* can do for *you*. For you are the one in trouble now."

CHAPTER 5

WOES OF AN ACCIDENTAL PRESIDENT

⟓⟐⟐⟐⟐⟐⟐⟐⟐

F ranklin Roosevelt had died at 4:45 PM, April 12, in Georgia. Harry Truman, absolutely dazed, waited to be sworn in, with Bess sniffling and Margaret unbelieving. A very worn Bible was found, and Truman became president at 7:09. He insisted on being called Harry S. Truman (no middle name) and kissed the Bible. Cabinet members said they had to talk to him right away. They had to wait. Instead, the family went to a neighbor's house, his apartment being known and unsecured by the Secret Service. Truman ate a turkey sandwich and slept soundly. At the East Room services for Roosevelt on April 14, Mrs. Roosevelt, after prayers, asked the bishop to pronounce FDR's most famous line when he was inaugurated during the greatest depression in history: "Let me assert my firm belief that the only thing we have to fear is fear itself." It was, once again, the perfect line for the moment, for only a few men knew Truman's qualities. He noticed that, when he entered the East Room for the service, no one stood up, an enormous discourtesy to a president. Truman took it lightly, but it seemed no one could yet parse that he was the president.

This was the second time a president acceded to the highest office in the midst of a great war, the Civil War barely being over with only a formal surrender signed as an enemy was still in the field in places, when Andrew Johnson took Lincoln's place. This time, the war was global, but, again, the new president was outside the circle of policy makers, as innocent as the proverbial baby. Everyone seemed to want instant decisions about momentous events unfolding at breakneck speed. Later, in 1948, Truman himself recalled what had been happening and recorded it in a letter to his sister, Mary: "Two wars were in progress—one in Europe and one in Asia. We were supporting both of them with men, munitions, planes and ships. . . . Between the two surrenders I went to Berlin to meet Stalin and Churchill. On that trip coming home I ordered the Atomic Bomb to be dropped on Hiroshima and Nagasaki. It was a terrible decision. But I made it. And I made it to save 250,000 boys from the United States and I'd make it again under similar circumstances."

Truman addressed Congress two days into his presidency. The members rose and gave him a tremendous ovation. (Was he home?) In a short, fifteen-minute speech—with applause stopping him seventeen times—he asked all to join him in finishing Roosevelt's work. A nice touch, and so the man overlooked at Roosevelt's memorial service in the White House was now recognized as the nation's, and the world's, leader. He would be Rooseveltian, following the party's much-admired leader. Truman's accent was unlike that of his great predecessor with his sonorous upper-class New York tones and broad a's. The new president's was flat and midwestern, with sharp *r*'s and not the soft, slurred, *r*'s of the New York and East Coast elite. The two Roosevelts had the same eastern, upper-class tones, only that Teddy was a tenor and Franklin a baritone. Truman's voice was like most Americans'. In this first showcase of his tenure, he pledged that the war would be vigorously pursued and the terms remained unconditional surrender. He would support a United Nations, fulfilling Woodrow Wilson's heart's desire, without mentioning his name. He ended by intoning one of his favorite prayers, King Solomon's: "Give therefore thy servant an understanding heart to judge my people, that I may discern between good and bad: for who is able to judge this thy so great people?" He closed with: "I ask only to be a good and faithful servant of my Lord and my people." It was a good beginning and a smooth transition.

Truman's first decision was to keep the American delegation on track to attend the important inaugural meeting of the United Nations, to be held in San Francisco. The UN would always be dear to his policy throughout his presidency. He believed that the country's spurning of the League of Nations after World War I had been a great mistake. Collective action in the early days of Hitler's rise and belligerency might have clipped his wings. President Hindenberg might have removed him from the chancellorship.

There was some gloom on the part of many major players when Truman ascended. Secretary of State Stettinius expected "cheap courthouse politics." The great fighting generals, Omar Bradley and George S. Patton Jr., did not know what to expect. Dwight Eisenhower was downbeat. Those who knew Truman from his experience in the Senate, however, were sanguine. Various politicos' responses to the great upheaval were interesting. John Nance Garner, Roosevelt's earlier vice president, found Truman "honest and patriotic." He had "guts" and "the stuff in him." Republican Senator Vandenberg of Michigan said: "He could swing the job." John J. McCloy, who held many posts in government over the years, said: "Oh, I felt good, because I *knew* him. I knew the kind of man he was." Assistant Secretary of State Dean Acheson said: "He was straightforward, decent, simple, entirely honest. . . . He will learn fast." Mamma said: "Harry will get along all right." Last, but not least, Jim Pendergast cabled his friend: "Get in there and pitch. You can handle it."

Truman was an early riser and got to the office at 9 AM sharp. The desk was cleared of all the gewgaws Roosevelt kept on it, as well as papers. He chose his own desk, the beautiful one given to Rutherford B. Hayes by Queen Victoria and made famous when both Roosevelts used it. It was made from timbers of the British Arctic exploration ship, the *Resolute,* which had been abandoned in 1854 and found by Americans the next year and returned. Roosevelt's pictures were gone. The new president preferred Remington to Currier and Ives. Truman sat in a big black chair in a green room, looking small, compared to his predecessor with his massive upper torso, the work of years of exercise to try to walk. To a reporter, he mused: "There have been few men in all history the equal of the man into whose shoes I am stepping. . . . I pray to God I can measure up to the task." Truman knew it was wise to be humble, given the huge reputation, deservedly, of Roosevelt, but he also knew he had enough confidence to take on the job, learn quickly, and do the right thing. Of all the jobs he had had, a few were good preparations, although he never dreamed he would be president. For example, his heroic service in the army and his superb handling of the investigation of defense expenditures gave him the steel he needed to face problems. And his disposition to delegate jobs to trusted associates and read all the papers put on his desk would help him. He may have been the first president, incidentally, who studied the nation's budget, that enormous mound of paper and obfuscation that Congress puts together each year. (Jimmy Carter, the engineer president, may have been the second president to try to master a federal budget of thousands of pages of paper.)

So serious was Truman about mastering the job that he quickly began suffering from overwork. He once told a friend that "the detail of this job is killing me." He slept for about six and a half hours a night, with a nap. Sometimes he went for a walk and swam in the White House pool. He set fixed meetings of all the cabinet members. These included Stettinius, State; Henry Morgenthau Jr., Treasury; Stimson, War; Francis Biddle, Justice; Frank Walker, Postmaster General; Frances Perkins, Labor; Henry Wallace, Commerce; Harold Ickes, Interior;

Claude Wickard, Agriculture; James Forrestal, Navy. He listened, took notes, and spoke up when necessary. He was methodical and liked memos, which he annotated. He loved jokes, and one of his favorites was: "There goes the Vice President, with nothing on his mind but the health of the President." He exhibited a wonderful sense of humor when he relaxed, to most politicians' surprise. (So few had known him, earlier, or had reached out to be friends.) But he couldn't fake it; when he smiled, one observer said, he looked "like a mule eating briars." He loved gossip, especially about his former congressional mates. His only hobby was talking about and following the weather. But his love of history often shone through, and he had a long letter-writing relationship with another lover of history, who was not an important figure, otherwise, in his life, about Roman generals and emperors like Hadrian, Trajan, Mark Antony, and Antoninus Pius and their doings, as well as about Charlemagne and Charles Martel, to name a few. He dipped into books sent to the White House—hundreds each year—by the American Booksellers Association. He was moved, emotionally, in the presence of war heroes and sniffled when the Chief Rabbi of Israel ended a meeting with a prayer thanking the Almighty for making Truman's existence possible.

Truman wrote personal letters—his mother or another member of his family heard from him just about every week. His mother died in 1947, but letters to the rest of the family continued. He signed about 600 others each day. He paid as much attention to congressional leaders as to those leading the war and making policy. These leading political figures could number 100 each week. He read his speeches to Bess for comments. His mother-in-law living with the Trumans did not change her mind about his not being good enough for Bess, as exhibited by her always calling him Mr. Truman. He adored his daughter, and that love was reciprocated. He called her affectionate names in letters, for too long calling her "baby," wanted her to write to him often, followed her formal education—she went to George Washington University, getting a degree in history—her piano playing and, later, her singing career of light opera and songs. He made clear, however, that he expected her to marry and give him grandchildren—and she did, four boys.

FIGURE 16 Portrait of Mrs. Bess Wallace Truman, First Lady, ca. 1945. *Credit:* Hessler Studio of Washington, DC, courtesy of the Harry S. Truman Library.

When fatigued, quite often, Truman was sent away by his doctor for rest, one favorite destination being Key West, but also Shangri La, Roosevelt's retreat in the Catoctin Mountains. There were no more psychosomatic illnesses. He was the master of himself, finally. But a new two-sidedness arose. He could be amiable and charming; or he could be livid and fantasizing, the latter in private letters and the former with close associates, who left memoirs about their mistakes. He loved people, but he never lost a bit of insecurity lurking inside that made him think he had been harsh with someone, when he really was just full of straight talk. He was a more complicated man than most writers who covered the White House were able to discover.

Truman began his presidency with two important decisions. On his first day, he asked Stettinius for a report on all diplomatic problems in Europe by the end of the day. He requested briefings on the war every day from Stimson, Marshall, Admiral William Leahy, and Forrestal, Admiral Ernest King, and Byrnes, the last a kind of de facto assistant president under Roosevelt, then Secretary of State under Truman from July 1945. (Stettinius became ambassador to the UN.) He wanted to know as much as they did; good and full information made for the best decision making. He would not be a chief left out of the inner circle. He visited Congress to lunch with friends, those from his senatorial days and the few who had been delirious when he, surprisingly, had won reelection to the Senate. He seemed "pale and tense," but who wouldn't be in the circumstances? He mentioned what a terrible job he had, and in memorable words blurted out: "I felt like the moon, the stars, and all the planets had fallen on me." Such a statement gave him a measure of grace with the press and the country as he gathered up the reins of government. It would be a mistake to think that he was either bewildered or frightened by the tasks before him. He was a sturdy politician, just startled by the sudden turn of events. The second decision was to ask the Secretary of the Treasury, Henry

Morgenthau, for a report on the nation's financial condition that day. He was a budget hawk for most of his presidency and would be pried loose from that position only under extreme circumstances.

Truman made a smooth transition to the presidency. Congress sensed that he was one of them and that they had as president their amiable and able friend. Truman's next act was personal, to move his family into the beautiful Blair House, across from the White House, in order to give Mrs. Roosevelt as much time as she needed to leave her home for so many years. She took about a month. There would also be time to paint and renovate the White House. Bess found the mansion dirty and shabby, with rats scurrying about. There was rot and broken furniture. She set about replacing furniture and drapes, having rooms painted or scrubbed, and making the place livable. Mrs. Roosevelt had never used the $50,000 Congress had given her to keep up the house. It seemed she cared little about housekeeping, cooking, or, years before, taking care of her children. The meals at the White House had been terrible, and her babies never got the love and attention they deserved. She never tried to learn lessons from her own broken childhood and resented any help or interference. (Her mother-in-law deserves more credit than history gives her to make up for Eleanor's deficiencies.)

The days flowed on, and Truman kept reaching out to the public, which didn't really know him, and to influentials via the newspapers. He held a press conference on April 17, with hundreds of reporters squeezing into his office. He appeared open and confident on many questions, and at the end of it, the re-porters literally applauded his performance. Truman had won over another important gaggle in Washington. Unlike Roo-sevelt, who entered his office between 10 and 10:30 AM, Tru-man was now at his desk even earlier than at first, at 8:30 AM. Reporters were stunned by the early hour; many had been out carousing the evening before, and knew a new man was in charge. George Elsey, who ran the White House Map Room, the international communications center, described the presi-dent as "alert, sharp . . . very vigorous, very strong." Medical and sartorial records show that the president was 5 foot 9 inches, chest 42.5 inches, waist 35.5 inches, shoe 9B, collar 15.5 inches, gloves 9 inches, and hat 7 and three-quarters. He was a compact man of great energy. No one at the White House was used to such activity and get-up-and-go in their president. Often, he was known to grab his hat and be off someplace. Of course, Roosevelt was never able to do so, and Hoover, Coolidge, and Harding had been sedentary men.

Truman brought a lot of old friends, many of them army buddies, into the White House, to the dismay of some White House watchers. One recalls a later president, John F. Kennedy, responding to comments about his bringing old friends into the office: "The presidency is not a place to make new friends." In Truman's case, some friends did not stay long. Even those who stayed did not rise to the level of praise. His soldier friend Harry Vaughan, whom Truman liked and trusted, could be thought of as the president's Falstaff. Truman was different from the men in government service who were eastern, wealthy, cultured, and assured. They went to the best boarding schools and the Ivy League colleges. Many knew each other. They were of the now Old Establishment. They mimicked Roosevelt. But Truman recognized the merits and strengths of Roosevelt's men and worked with them. Some he even got to like. (But he was uncomfortable having a woman in the cabinet, and the first to serve in any cabinet, Secretary of Labor Frances Perkins, whom FDR had appointed in 1933, did not stay long.) The men accepted various assignments, whether it was Dean Acheson; Robert Lovett, a man for all seasons; Charles Bohlen; John J. McCloy, a poor boy whose talent made him rich; or James Forrestal, among others. Some lived in European-style castles on thousands of acres, in or near Washington, others ran wealthy law firms with international clients. They were seasoned and eager to help the new president. Most of them didn't know him personally or, indeed, anything about his middling origins or pretensions and his high-school-only background.

Truman's cabinet was a mixture of friends and old hands: Tom Clark as attorney general, Lewis Schwellenbach as Secretary of Labor, Clinton Anderson as Agriculture Secretary, Jimmy Byrnes as Secretary of State, Bob Hannegan as Postmaster General, and old-timers Henry Wallace at Commerce, Harold Ickes at Interior, Henry Morgenthau at Treasury, and Stimson as Secretary of War. There have been more distinguished cabinets in history, but since the Founding Fathers, the quality has varied. In one way, Truman's cabinet was fortunate, as he met with them frequently and listened. He was like a sponge absorbing as much information as he could, and with his excellent memory he retained most of it. Most recent cabinets had been window dressing and not organized to present or reflect a president's program but represented interests Congress favored. Roosevelt had almost never convened the body.

On July 15, Truman took out a yellowed piece of paper that he had carried in his wallet since the age of ten and read it to a reporter. It was from "Locksley Hall" by Alfred Lord Tennyson, published in 1842:

> For I dipt into the future, far as human eye could see,
> Saw the Vision of the world, and all the wonder that would be;
>
> Saw the heavens fill with commerce, argosies of magic sails,
> Pilots of the purple twilight, dropping down with costly bales;
>
> Heard the heavens fill with shouting and there rain'd a ghastly dew
> From the nation's airy navies grappling in the central blue: . . .
>
> Till the war-drum throbb'd no longer and the battle-flags were furl'd
> In the Parliament of man, the Federation of the world.

Truman said this writing was only a poet's dream and that, today, it seemed as if that dream would come true. When the story was published, the European war was over, and Truman was optimistic. How wrong he was. It was time to throw away his boyhood ideal. The Asian war was burning up a continent and was soon to face a holocaust of cinders and ash made of bodies. The war in the Pacific was a series of bloody battles to take islands away from the Japanese army—which fought to the last man—in order to build bases from which long-range American bombers could pummel the Japanese homeland. Guadalcanal, Tarawa, Iwo Jima, and other names scarred memories, and thousands of American soldiers and marines died or were seriously wounded there. Then the systematic bombing of Japan began, and the largest cities were burned out by bombs and incendiaries. Tokyo, for example, was subjected to such raids, and 100,000 people were killed in one night. In Europe, the German government surrendered in May 1945. That historic battleground of so many wars over the centuries was now an unbelievable pile of rubble, with survivors starving. The American army had stopped before Berlin, as arranged in conferences, and the Soviet army fought house-to-house to subdue it. It looked like a moonscape when the last shot was fired. Hitler had committed suicide, rather than face capture, and the Allied armies met and celebrated the hard-fought victory. Secondaries signed the unconditional surrender.

There is no more contentious issue in Truman's presidency than his decision to use the atom bomb against Japan. On August 2, 1939, Albert Einstein had written to Roosevelt informing him that a momentously powerful bomb could be built. He was referring to a purified uranium-235 blast. It would be an atomic bomb, thereafter called the Gadget. Until 1941, little money was given to such a project. On November 6, 1941, Dr. Vannevar Bush, director of the Office of Scientific Research and Development (OSRD), visited Secretary of War Stimson, bringing a report by the National Academy of Sciences that stated that it would be possible to build "a fission bomb of superlatively destructive power" within three or four years. Dr. James Bryant Conant, head of the National Defense Research Committee (NDRC), lobbied to begin work. Stimson reacted to the news of November 6 with the notation of "a most terrible thing" in his diary. Roosevelt encouraged the effort with a Top Policy Group of Stimson, Wallace, and Marshall to speed ahead. It was decided to give the project to the army, under Stimson, who did not object, although his whole career, up to now, was one of trying to harness the indiscriminate instruments of war—like submarines—and to make peace through treaties, like the Kellogg-Briand Pact, both failures in their peace intentions. Stimson's was a deeply held philosophical and pragmatic life mission, and the irony is that he was now responsible for manufacturing what was up to that time the most destructive weapon in history.

The building of the bomb would mean establishing huge industrial plants, the unraveling of the secrets of uranium and plutonium, and the bringing together of thousands of the best scientists and workers, all in secret. The appropriations were hidden in the federal budget, the very appropriations Senator Truman had tried to ferret out when he headed the special investigation of defense spending and Stimson told him to butt out and called him a nuisance. The total cost eventually would be $2 billion—a very large sum in prewar dollars, perhaps twenty times that in today's dollars—and hard-charging General Leslie Groves was to run the project at Los Alamos in New

Mexico and other places. Stimson did and didn't watch over the project, as he was busy winning a war, but called the bomb "diabolical," when he was brought in on the project. Truman learned about the bomb after he became president, and, like others, deferred asking how it was being built—scientifically, that is—and what it was intended to do, specifically. All was left to J. Robert Oppenheimer, director of the project, and his crew.

There are two questions about Truman's culpability, if such a word ought, ever, to be used at all, regarding the use of the atomic bomb. One, was his directive that it was to be used only on military targets followed? Two, did he know the true devastation wrought by the by-product, radiation sickness? The second question is more easily disposed of: the answer is no. There were some warnings from scientists familiar with the project and radiation's effect, but few if any others knew of this deadly possibility in calculations, even after the actual, enormous test blast in the New Mexico desert on July 16, 1945. Radiation was a concern, but what could be done, if anything? General Groves himself was not troubled and thought that atom bombs could be used to prepare the battlefield before an American invasion of Japan and troops could advance within a half hour of the blast!

Roosevelt had been silent and delayed any decision on the bomb's use, although, among policy makers, it had been decided that it would be used on Germany, if ready in time. Stimson reported that trying to get Roosevelt to decide on important matters was like "chasing a vagrant beam of sunshine around a vacant room." It was a nice poetic phrase, but Stimson was dealing with deadly matters, and the aging Secretary of War, plagued with heart problems, should have been more energetic and purposeful on this momentous issue. Deadly questions were on the table and not in the penumbra when Truman became president. Whether Stimson was up to the job is an unanswered question. As it turned out, the secretary, fighting two major wars, put off decisions on the atomic bomb until it was too late to change the bomb's blast construction and use. But several other options had been on the table: demonstrating the power of the bomb on a deserted island, or bombing peripheral Japanese military installations, or just plain telling Japan about the incredible power of the bomb before actual use. There were committees set up on policy and targeting at work on such problems, along with policy experts, and reports passed around among top officials and Truman. Only the president could decide on the use of the bomb.

What had not been known by policy makers, or Truman, was that, all along, Oppenheimer and the scientists were developing a special-type bomb, one beyond the thousand or so pounds of explosives encased in conventional bombs. The bomb would have the power of a small sun. The secrets of atoms, the elemental forms of life, would be blasted open. Oppenheimer made it known that any demonstration that was picayune, or away from the Japanese homeland, would not be sufficient to make Japan surrender. He was making the ultimate weapon to destroy cities and kill civilians. Oppenheimer considered the ideal targets to be large cities, three miles or more in diameter, that had not already been hit with conventional bombs. There were several possibilities, but Hiroshima was chosen as the best target. It was located on a broad flat delta on the Ota River, twenty-six square miles. Seventy-five percent of Hiroshima's population was located in the heavily built-up area in the center of the city. It contained the Second Army Headquarters, which commanded the defense of southern Japan. It was also a communications headquarters, a storage point, and an assembly area for troops. The city, as a whole, was highly susceptible to fire damage. Population was 380,000. It was considered a city of considerable military importance, although in later accounts this judgment was in dispute. Stimson and others did not find the time to understand the trajectory this work had taken, and they decided, wrongly, that targets could be chosen late in the game. As General Groves observed, Truman was "like a little boy on a toboggan who never had an opportunity to say yes. All he could say was no."

The second target, Nagasaki, was the best natural harbor on Kyushu, the island chosen as the first site for an invasion. The heavily built-up part of the city was about four square miles of a total of thirty-five. The city was the home of ordnance, ships, military equipment, and other war materials. Wooden buildings held most people and industries, closely packed together. Population was 240,000.

By May 1945, there was no turning back on the nature of the bomb or the negotiation of targets. Kyoto and Tokyo had been taken off the target list, the first because Stimson knew it as a jewel of a city, the second because it was already devastated and therein resided the government that would need to surrender formally. Truman, Stimson, and Marshall clung to the now-quaint view that civilians were not being targeted. A school of revisionists arose a generation after the atomic bomb was used and secret papers were made available that argue that there was no need to use the bomb, as Japan was trying to end the war. This is a discussable view, within the large context of the war, but untenable, as will be shown.

A deadly game was unfolding, at that time, that made conventional bombing and Okinawa-type warfare seem like small events, and there were other issues also on the table. Truman was at Potsdam in July 1945 and was dismayed about how Poland was being lost to the Soviets, but it was suggested that he now focus on Japan and not start a row with Stalin. Stalin was ill and delayed arriving. Truman decided to use the extra day to travel by car to Berlin to survey the damage and learn what conventional bombing had achieved. The devastation was appalling, and people seemed almost not human in their wretchedness. One historian has suggested that no other American president ever witnessed such destruction and destitution, but perhaps he forgot Lincoln's visit to Richmond in 1865. And, of course, Truman had seen the frightening outcomes on people and the land from his World War I experiences. He recorded after his Berlin visit: "I thought of Carthage, Baalbeck, Jerusalem, Rome, Atlantis, Peking, Babylon, Nineveh; Scipio, Rameses II, Titus, Hermann [Arminius], Sherman, Jenghis Khan, Alexander, Darius the Great.... I hope for some sort of peace.... We are only termites on a planet and maybe when we bore too deeply into the planet there'll [be] a reckoning—who knows?"

The top policy makers had been schizoid about the use of the bomb and the morality of the terror. They wanted to be better than the Nazis, whose genocidal and beyond-brutal war was well-known. When Byrnes became Secretary of State on July 3, 1945, he tilted affairs toward a hard line against Japan. Truman had tried to be forceful about not wanting women and children targeted, but, at Potsdam, he made it known that he wanted the war to end as soon as possible. On May 16, 1945, he had agreed with Stimson that "the same rules of sparing the civilian population should be applied as far as possible to the use of any new weapons." He and Stimson had accepted the vague assurances that military targets only were chosen. If any blame was ever to be assessed, and this has been an ongoing historical game for over sixty years, it would be on the civilians who made the decisions leading to the use of atomic weapons. It was their responsibility to know what was going on in the laboratories and in the consulting committees. The lure of atomic power was mesmerizing, the diplomatic channels muddy, the failure to oversee targeting, early on, a grave mistake. But a major question must be asked: Should not the saving of perhaps hundreds of thousands of American soldiers' lives be put on history's scale?

Truman's and Stimson's orders were parsed by the policy makers and scientists at Los Alamos so that targets were chosen with some military installations on the periphery. The Target Committee, earlier set up, was explicit about how the atomic bomb would be most effective. It was as though the scientists and policy makers involved were riding on a parallel track with the president and his men. Oppenheimer's team and the Target Committee decided that an undamaged city was to be chosen, a firestorm was expected, and the degree or effects of radiation were questionable. The size of the blast was the main concern. The bomb was to be targeted at the center of the chosen, large city, as perfectly as the atmosphere and the bombsight would allow. The best results would be on targets with wooden houses and not concrete installations. The atomic bomb would be dropped by a plane at 30,000 feet, and exploded in the air, forty-three seconds after release, and the plane was to fly away as fast as possible to avoid the blast. In fact, the plane used over Hiroshima, the *Enola Gay*, was shaken by the blast, it was so powerful.

There are several descriptions of an atomic bomb explosion. All horrific. One of these, the first, is enough to forever imprint the catastrophe. William L. Laurence, formerly at the *New York Times,* but sent as a War Department historian, gave us his recollection on September 26, 1945, about the Trinity explosion in New Mexico on July 16, 1945, that was detonated just above land, in a tower:

> At that great moment in history, ranking with the moment in the long ago when man first put fire to work for him and started on his march to civilization, the vast energy locked within the hearts of the atoms of matter was released for the first time in a burst of flame such as had never before been seen on this planet, illuminating earth and sky for a brief span that seemed eternal with the light of many supersuns.

The elemental flame, the first ever made on the earth that did not have its origin in the sun, came from the explosion of the first atomic bomb. It was a full-dress rehearsal preparation of use of the bomb over Hiroshima and Nagasaki. . . .

It was a sunrise such as the world had never seen, a great green supersun climbing in a fraction of a second to a height of more than 8,000 feet, rising ever higher until it touched the clouds, lighting up the earth and sky all around with a dazzling luminosity.

Up it went, a great ball of fire about a mile in diameter, changing colors as it kept shooting upward, from deep purple to orange, expanding, growing bigger, rising as it was expanding, an elemental force freed from its bonds after being chained for billions of years.

For a fleeting instance the color was unearthly green, such as one sees only in the corona of the sun during total eclipse.

It was as though the earth had opened up and the skies had split. One felt as though he had been privileged to witness the Birth of the World—to be present at the moment of the Creation when the Lord said: Let there be light.

Such language would not be used again in describing the atomic bomb. It was an Epiphany, the magic of pure science before it was put to use. Witnessing the Trinity explosion, Oppenheimer—father of the bomb, mystic and poet, who knew what the near future of the explosion would be when fully mastered—remembered thinking about a line from the *Bhagavad Gita:* "Now I am become death, the destroyer of the worlds."

The director of the test took a less mythic tone when he said to Oppenheimer: "Now we are all sons of bitches."

The first question about hitting only military targets with atom bombs is a more difficult story to unravel. Where was the moral threshold in this first-ever military Armageddon? In both Germany and Japan, conventional bombing had destroyed cities and killed hundreds of thousands of civilians. In Japan 9 million persons had been made homeless. About 187,000 civilians had been killed and 214,000 injured. Cities such as Osaka, Yokohama, Nagoya, and Kobe were mostly destroyed. By October 1944, there were no significant industrial targets left to bomb. A naval blockade blocked oil and other imports. Food was running out. Only civilian targets were left, and Allied governments had approved these slaughters of peoples. (It should not be forgotten that Germany began civilian bombing in Spain and England.) When the bomb wasn't ready to use in Germany, Japan was targeted. Neither Roosevelt nor Truman ever questioned that it would be used when ready. Another question is often raised: Was there a difference between types of bombs, when almost equal numbers of people were casualties? One scientist rebuked the "tender souls" worrying about the use of the atomic bomb. Truman jotted down in his diary on June 17, 1945: "I have to decide Japanese strategy—shall we invade Japan proper or shall we [conventionally] bomb and blockade. That is my hardest decision to date. But I'll make it when I have all the facts." This was about a month before the first atomic Gadget was successfully exploded in the sands of New Mexico and Truman was told on July 16. A working bomb would be ready in early August.

FIGURE 17 *From left to right:* British Prime Minister Winston Churchill, President Harry S. Truman, and Soviet leader Joseph Stalin in the garden of the Cecilienhof Palace in Potsdam, Germany, July 25, 1945, during the Potsdam Conference. *Credit:* US Army Signal Corps, courtesy of the Harry S. Truman Library.

By July 25, Truman had made his decision and directed Stimson to use the bomb on Japanese military targets and soldiers and sailors, not women and children. The warning to the Japanese would be the Potsdam Declaration Defining Terms for Japanese Surrender, issued the next day. Eisenhower did not favor the use of the atomic bomb and later explained that it was a personal view, as he thought Japan was already defeated. Marshall thought use of the bomb would save a quarter of a million American casualties. Leaders took the new president seriously. General Bradley called Truman "direct, unpretentious, clear thinking, and forceful." At Potsdam, Churchill found Truman a man of "exceptional character," not knowing that Truman found him long-winded. Moreover, Churchill favored using the bomb. When he learned of the successful test in the New Mexico sands, he coined another memorable phrase: "This atomic bomb is the Second Coming in Wrath."

After the Hiroshima bomb was unleashed on August 6, Truman issued a public statement: "The Japanese began the war from the air at Pearl Harbor. They have been repaid many fold. . . . If they do not now accept our terms [unconditional surrender], they may expect a rain of ruin from the air, the like of which has never been seen on this earth." The full dimensions of the war Japan rained on Asia were a part of the hard decision to get an unconditional surrender. Japan was viewed as a brutal enemy and menace to Asia. In a nutshell, Japan had taken 150 times more Asian lives in its imperial wars since 1931 than the United States took in its atomic bombing of Hiroshima and Nagasaki. Japan had attacked and occupied a far larger part of the world than did Germany and its European allies. One historian writes: "There was a holocaust. A great devastation, a reckless destruction of life in Asia."

Manchuria in 1931, China in 1937, Indochina in 1940, Malaya, Thailand, Burma, Hong Kong, Singapore, the Philippines (an American protectorate), Borneo, the East Indies, and New Guinea were all conquered, devastated, their people brutalized, women raped, prisoners starved, beaten, killed, even flayed. About 24 million people were killed and 100 million injured—a number equal to the population of the United States at the time. The Japanese government and military rivaled the

Nazis in their war crimes. Japanese armed forces suffered severe casualties, but not until 1945 were the home islands and civilians targeted for destruction. "How would we remember the war if we had been invaded and suffered the equivalent of one '9/11' per day—every day—on average, from 1941 to 1945?" a historian of the war asks. "That is what happened to our Asian Allies." Every week that the war continued saw mounting casualties. Japan would not surrender because it had never lost a war. The use of the atomic bomb may have saved from one million to three million lives and many more wounded.

Americans remember the hard words of General Sherman of Civil War fame, who said, "War is hell" when he marched through Georgia to the sea, destroying everything valuable in a twenty-mile swath. George Elsey, Truman's aide, reflected at the time of unleashing the atomic bombs: "It is all well and good to come along and say the bomb was a horrible thing. The whole goddamn war was a horrible thing."

Truman was not shown the pictures of what occurred in Hiroshima as soon as they were available. On August 9, he made another public statement. This is an excerpt: "The world will note that the first atomic bomb was dropped on Hiroshima, a military base. That was because we wished in this first attack to avoid, insofar as possible, the killing of civilians. But that attack is only a warning of things to come. If Japan does not surrender, bombs will have to be dropped on her war industries and, unfortunately, thousands of civilian lives will be lost. I urge Japanese civilians to leave industrial cities immediately, and save themselves from destruction."

Truman did not know that, from the beginning, scientists were creating a bomb that could only show its massive destruction on intact cities, incinerating buildings and people. And Oppenheimer had planned it that way. There are later, interesting, recollections by Truman. In his *Memoirs* he wrote: "The final decision of where and when to use the atomic bomb was up to me. Let there be no mistake about that. I regarded the bomb as a military weapon and never had any doubt that it should be used. The top military advisers to the President recommended its use, and when I talked to Churchill he unhesitatingly told me that he favored the use of the atomic bomb if it might aid to end the war." Truman also wrote: "It occurred to me that a quarter of a million of the flower of our young manhood were worth a couple of Japanese cities and I still think they were and are." It is true, and understandable, that Truman did not sleep well the night when he decided to use the bomb—July 24. We also know that headaches returned for days, and he was physically not well. Bess, after two months in Independence, hurried to Washington. The Japanese still not surrendering, Truman ordered conventional bombing to resume on the 13th. It did. But, at that point, he also took back total command of atomic bombing directly from the army, which had received its orders through Secretary of War Stimson. There would be no more of that kind of total annihilation while he was president. It is interesting that atomic weapons never did fall into the hands of the military, again, but were securely held by succeeding presidents.

The war against Imperial Japan continued, and Truman held to his terms of unconditional surrender. He held even when told—never by an official of the Japanese government but only by men with no influence or by vague intercepts—that the Japanese only wanted to keep the emperor (considered a divine figure but also the head of the whole military-political mechanism that was Japan), and when other terms, never put in official communiqués, were suggested. No official message from Japan even hinted that Japan was ready to surrender under any circumstances. As late as July 1945, the Japanese foreign minister wrote: "We are not asking [for] the Russian's mediation in anything like unconditional surrender." Truman's sentiment toward Japan was penned in his diary, August 11: "When you have to deal with a beast you have to treat him as a beast. It is most regrettable but nevertheless true."

It has been argued by revisionist historians that the atom bomb was really used as a diplomatic weapon against the Soviet Union, which was flouting one of the elements of the Yalta Agreements, that of setting up democratic governments in Eastern Europe and the Baltic States. Other elements of that set of agreements were the establishment of areas of occupation by America, England, France, and the USSR, with Berlin divided among the four war partners, which was happening. But Poland became an issue, as communists were taking over the government, and the Allies wanted some kind of diplomatic weapon to thwart this happening. Also, revisionists state that the United States did not want the Soviets to join the war against Japan too soon; that is, Truman wanted to use his atomic bombs first, as weapons of intimidation, generally. This revisionist history has been adequately disputed by historians, but no account of the use of atomic weapons ought to exclude mentioning it.

When the Allied leaders met in Potsdam in July 1945, President Truman was anxious to get Stalin to agree to join the UN, along with his entering the war against Japan. In the negotiations, the inexperienced president, inadvertently, traded Poland for the UN because he made no objection to communists taking over the fledgling government. Truman wanted Stalin to be receptive to what he himself wanted, most of all. It was an unwise, ill-considered move, for Stalin didn't care about the UN, but he did want Poland and a piece of Asia and economic trade, as well as security on his borders, which meant control of his neighbors in a tight, military, sphere of influence. This big picture eluded Truman. The Soviet Union had lost 20 million souls in the war and was devastated up to the environs of Moscow. Stalin was determined to get reparations and security. He blithely stated that any government not fascist was democratic! Americans, following the Yalta Agreements, withdrew their troops 150 miles to the west, leaving the Russians their recognized sphere, then demobilized their army so fast that there was no punch in any future disputes with the Soviets. The Western Allies had no bargaining chips to counter aggressive Soviet moves.

Looking back, it could be argued that Roosevelt was somewhat taken in at Yalta—he was ill with congestive heart failure—and, now, Truman, the novice—was taken in by "Uncle Joe's" amiability. Truman thought Stalin could be reasoned with. Wasn't he just like Pendergast? But, domestic politicos do not translate diplomatically, and joviality was not a diplomatic tool. Truman got the least of the bargain.

When Truman implied to Stalin at Potsdam that he had a new, momentous weapon, Stalin showed little interest—his spies had already informed him about the atomic bomb—and it played no part in Truman's negotiations. Since the president only wanted Russia to enter the war against Japan and join the UN, he thought the conference a success. Yalta and Potsdam, most historians agree, were Allied wins. But were they entirely? The Soviet Union under Stalin had already allowed millions of its people to starve to death in the Ukraine in the 1930s, had tried and killed top military officers on trumped-up charges in 1938, killed off the Polish military, political, and intellectual elite in the forests of Katyn—perhaps more than 10,000 men— were treating war prisoners brutally, and did not object to Jews being corralled, gassed, and burned in industrial furnaces. How could Stalin be seen as an honest, trusted partner?

The Western Allies saved half of Germany and most of Berlin for freedom and democracy. The Baltic states and Eastern Europe were yoked to despotic communist governments. All this does not mean that the Allies should have declared war on Russia in 1945, as some military men like George Patton wanted, but only that Truman, and the new prime minister of Great Britain, Clement Attlee (Churchill was defeated in the recent election), did not negotiate as successfully for the immediate future of Europe as it should have been possible. The staunch pessimist on the Soviets, Churchill, was gone and sorely missed. His unforgettable phrase that an Iron Curtain was descending on Europe was both a prophecy and a curse. George Kennan, the best Russian expert in the government, and Averell Harriman, who held many posts, including ambassador to the Soviet Union, were sure Russia would not keep any bargains. Truman, too confident of his negotiating skills, did not use their expertise. Kennan despaired and thought Truman naïve. Harriman, a skilled and tough negotiator, resigned, because the new Secretary of State, Byrnes, did not consult him. Only a dozen years later did Truman face the truth that he had been naïve, "an innocent idealist," and Stalin, an "unconscionable Russian dictator." He also wrote, in a schizoid statement: "I liked the little son of a bitch." (Stalin was only 5 foot 5 inches.) It is hard to understand such contrary statements.

The horror of Hiroshima and Nagasaki was soon getting worldwide attention, and the new holocaust was beginning to sink into an uneasy consciousness. The Hiroshima bomb of August 6 leveled sixty percent of the city, everything within a mile of the blast destroyed, almost everything within 4.4 miles burned out, with 100,000 casualties, or almost one quarter of the city's population killed and an additional one quarter seriously injured. Radiation injuries were instantaneous and severe, with horrific burns and skin often hanging gruesomely from bodies. Nagasaki was also destroyed within a radius of a mile. Three square miles were devastated. Huge steel works and the torpedo plant were no more. There were 70,000 deaths. Reports on the two bomb explosions later told that effects from radiation were due to instantaneous discharge of gamma radiation at the moment of explosion and not to persistent radioactivity. The burns were widespread and "flash" burns prevalent. A comparison is often made with the March 1945 conventional bombing of Tokyo, which had burned out 41.5 percent of the city, with 100,000 casualties. In the battles of Iwo Jima and Okinawa, there were about 61,000 American casualties. In comparison, 42,000 American casualties were reported in the Normandy battle. The destruction of all such life, so casually recorded, was mind-boggling, when not sickening.

As it turned out, the UN was a fledgling organization, full of *nyets* by the Soviets in the Security Council. International cooperation to cap atomic use was slow to materialize—Stalin was busy making his own bomb and did not want to be hampered. At the same time, Stalin was denied any benefit from warring against Japan—the war ended too soon for him—and this started another dispute with the Allies.

The game changer in the Asian war was, of course, the atomic bomb. It is not true, as some have contended, that the United States had only two atomic bombs, and so needed to get a quick response from Japan. A third bomb was awaiting an order to be sent to Tinian Island in the Marianas, where the bombs were assembled. And as many as ten bombs were in the works. As much ink has been spilled on these two devastating atomic events as on the morality of making the bomb itself and how it was decided to be used. After the Hiroshima bomb was dropped, there was disbelief as to whether it was something new. No Japanese suspected anything more than a conventional bomb. A military officer was sent to investigate, however, and reported back in a day that it was an atomic bomb. The second blast then occurred. Nagasaki damage was about half of that of Hiroshima. Actually it was a plutonium bomb, a more sophisticated atomic weapon, that was dropped.

Should the allies have waited for a response after Hiroshima? Was it true that the Japanese were expected to fight to the last man, regardless of new, devastating weapons, as Paul Nitze—director of the US Strategic Bombing Survey, published in 1946—and others claimed? When policy makers surveyed the landscape before the bomb was exploded, they calculated that by the summer of 1945, the United States had suffered 1,250,000 combat-related casualties worldwide. An even more bitter fight than that against Germany was expected. Truman knew the European casualty figures. His Joint War Plans Committee was preparing estimates regarding an invasion of Japan in their June 1945 meetings. They were wildly diverse. He was given a figure of 31,000 casualties, in the first three days of invasion. There is no evidence that Truman ever received information from military officials that an invasion of Japan would cost as many as 500,000 to 1 million American casualties or deaths, as he and some of his advisers claimed after the war. This was one of the most contentious issues regarding Truman's wartime tenure. At several points, we must ask: What did he know, and when did he know it?

Truman was then told that Japan could muster 5 million men. Thousands of kamikaze planes were being readied for suicide bombings. All Japanese were told to defend themselves, even if only with bamboo sticks. Early casualty estimates soon changed, with 400,000 to 800,000 Americans falling. Herbert Hoover, asked to weigh in, calculated a loss of a million Americans. Marshall estimated a quarter million deaths and injuries. Some casualty figures were based on recent figures from the invasions of Luzon and then Iwo Jima and Okinawa; in the latter two, the Japanese fought to the last man, as they were ordered not to surrender. Truman told the military that he did not want an Okinawa from one end of Japan to the other. More than 115,000 American prisoners were starving to death and being brutalized. The Japanese threatened to massacre them. At the time, in July, the Joint Chiefs of Staff did not consider conventional bombing and naval blockade to be a strong alternative to using an atomic bomb in the making, a fast way to end the war. Marshall thought both an invasion and the use of any new bomb would be necessary. The invasion plan was set for November 1.

Would Truman have proceeded toward using the bomb even if he had known the worst-case scenarios? His stated aim, over and again, was to end the war as quickly as possible. A good historian, especially of the Civil War—General Lee was his all-time favorite military leader—Truman must have known that in that great war for the Union and to end slavery, 600,000 soldiers were killed, sometimes in battles claiming tens of thousands of casualties. The aggressive General Ulysses S. Grant—Lincoln's favorite officer—was the great soldier-killer, but Lee had also launched battles with thousands of casualties. Truman, like Lincoln, anguished over great losses of men. The artillery captain in World War I cried when he lost one soldier in his battery, and not even from war wounds. When Truman made the decision not to use the atom bomb again, he famously said: "I didn't want all those kids killed." And recall he, himself, became ill when making the decision to use the bomb, rushing Bess to his side from Independence. He was all too human.

Japan was only indicating through informal channels and to the Soviets that it sought a mediated peace, not a surrender. Could the United States deal with that? Italy was allowed to end its war conditionally. But Japan had a different fighting spirit, and its terms, not always specific in its communications even to its own ambassadors and insiders, seemed to be: no large-scale occupation, their own war crimes trials, control over their own disarmament, and the keeping of the emperor, which meant the military-political system that led to war. It would only give up its empire. No message from Japan even hinted that it was ready to surrender under any circumstances.

The Potsdam Declaration was firm on the emperor, and the military-political system reigning in his name, and Japanese officials: "There must be eliminated for all time the authority and influence of those who have deceived and misled the people of Japan into embarking on world conquest. . . . Stern justice shall be meted out to all war criminals."

A bit earlier, some policy makers—McCloy, Joseph Grew (who had been ambassador to Japan until Pearl Harbor), and General MacArthur—thought the United States did not mean to abolish the position of emperor. MacArthur had warned in 1944 that "to dethrone, or hang, the Emperor would cause a tremendous and violent reaction from all Japanese. . . . Hanging of the Emperor to them would be compared to the crucifixion of Christ to us. All would fight to die like ants."

Truman's thinking was that Japan had attacked the United States and it showed itself to be beyond brutal in its treatment of prisoners of war. The Bataan Death March was imprinted on every American soul. In March 1942, when Bataan in the Philippines fell, 12,000 Americans and 63,000 Filipinos were captured and marched seventy-six miles in extreme heat without food or water to a POW camp. They were beaten and shot along the way. Up to 10,000 died. Some estimates were as high as 20,000 dead after internment in wretched conditions. It is worth repeating the war's horrors. There were refinements of inhumanity in the treatment of those thrown upon the mercy of the Japanese military. Sadism was institutional. Prisoners of war and civilian internees were starved, raped, bayoneted, beheaded, and, in some cases, vivisected. Japanese madness brought out American ruthlessness. All this and American racism only led to the fixed demand of unconditional surrender.

Truman wrote in 1945 on why he used the atomic bomb. "We have used it in order to shorten the agony of war, in order to save lives of thousands and thousands of young Americans." The most powerful man in Congress, Senator Richard B. Russell Jr. of Georgia, advised Truman after atomic bombs were unleashed that he should keep going with all available weapons; the object was to save American lives. Finally it was up to one person to end the war: the Japanese emperor. He ordered his government to surrender. He argued that not to do so "would reduce the nation to ashes. We must bear the unbearable." He told his cabinet: "It is my desire that you, my Ministers of State, accede to my wishes and forthwith accept the Allied reply [to surrender]." Japan's war minister committed suicide. The emperor's action gave him a bit of credit with the Allies, and he was allowed to stay on his throne but was subject to the Supreme Allied

Commander. He was made a figurehead, and not even a constitutional monarchy was allowed.

Truman held a press conference on August 14 to announce Japan's acceptance of the unconditional surrender peace terms. The White House swarmed with people out from Lafayette Park across Pennsylvania Avenue. With Bess in tow, Harry walked out on the lawn and gave the V sign to the jubilant crowds. He later reemerged to say a few words: "This is the day when Fascism and police government cease in the world." The sentimental and caring president telephoned Mrs. Roosevelt to tell her that he wished the great news had been announced by her husband.

The emperor proved to be a calming influence on the Japanese to accept the inevitable. But it should not be forgotten that the Japanese leaders were responsible for the lion's share of what befell their country. And secret intelligence communications, MAGIC and Ultra, clearly show the leaders' culpability. The story concludes with a peacetime success. The occupation and rehabilitation of Japan went more smoothly than that of Germany because Russia played no part and MacArthur was a skillful diplomat-soldier. In fact, it was a brilliant success. MacArthur democratized the country, pushed economic advance, and led it back to the community of nations.

Appropriately, in light of President Truman's home state, the peace treaty between the United States and Japan was signed on September 2, 1945, aboard the mighty battleship the USS *Missouri*.

CHAPTER 6

WINNING IS
EVERYTHING

A fter the war ended, the world was in chaos, still full of violence; famine stalked countries; and the Soviet Union
had captured its neighbors in its communist net. Truman
learned that agreements with Stalin meant nothing. The president wanted nations to be free, to schedule elections, to rebuild,
with help from the Allies. He had delegated diplomacy to his
short-tempered, undereducated Secretary of State, Jimmy
Byrnes, who was to implement his program. But Byrnes flew
by the seat of his pants in all matters needing attention. He told
the president that he was tired of "Russian deceits." On his own,
without informing Truman and without due planning, Byrnes
called a conference to meet in Moscow to discuss postwar Europe. He ignored the old hands, like Averell Harriman and
George Kennan, who knew more than he did about the Soviets.
In his diary on December 19, 1945, Kennan wrote about
Byrnes: "He plays his negotiations by ear, going into them with

no clear or fixed plan, with no definite set of objectives or limitations. He relies entirely on his own agility and presence of mind and hopes to take advantage of tactical openings."Kennan observed that Byrnes wanted some kind of agreement for domestic political reasons: Byrnes wanted to be president after Truman. Much of the Moscow conference concerned nations like Korea, Rumania, and Iran, which Byrnes knew nothing about and cared nothing for. All the problems were severe, and varied from country to country, but Byrnes treated them all like peas in a pod. For example, Koreans wanted a united country, Rumanians wanted to be free of Soviet intervention, and Iranians had oil, coveted by all countries, but were enmeshed in British imperial politics, and not free. And there were a score of other nations, or would-be nations, needing direction and assistance.

Furthermore, Byrnes did not send daily reports to Truman, as was customary and necessary. Not until December 24 did Truman learn what was going on. He received Byrnes's communiqué on the Moscow conference after newspapers had gotten it. It turns out the Moscow conference was lopsided in Moscow's favor, as the West recognized new communist governments in Bulgaria and Rumania, established a UN atomic energy commission, and gave Russia a presence in Asia. Despite these extraordinary agreements, Truman remained cordial toward Byrnes—he was always unwilling to have face-to-face confrontations with aides—but began to question his sagacity. He was unwilling even to discuss how he felt about the Moscow conference because he did not want to open a breach with

Byrnes. In a letter to his secretary, which he never sent, but saved for posterity, Truman revealed his mindset: "There isn't a doubt in my mind that Russia intends an invasion of Turkey and the seizure of the Black Sea Straits to the Mediterranean. Unless Russia is faced with an iron fist and strong language another war is in the making. . . . I'm tired of babying the Soviets."

By 1946, Truman and most other Americans believed the Soviet Union under Stalin was belligerent, totalitarian, and imperialistic. Stalin ranted at the West. Truman received a letter from Kennan warning that the Soviet Union was not amenable to change, and the president began to agree with him. The Soviets continued their imperialist drives toward Turkey and Iran. Byrnes's response was now tough, and Truman thought it right.

At Truman's behest, Churchill accepted an invitation by a Missouri college to address the students and receive an honorary degree on March 5, 1946. No topic was mentioned. Thus, the great former prime minister gave one of his most memorable speeches in Fulton, Missouri. He told his audience and, hence, the world, that Russia was lowering an Iron Curtain across Europe. He foresaw an inevitable East-West clash. Truman, on the platform, nodded in agreement. Yet the president was not ready, openly, to embrace publicly the English leader's truculent view. Nor was Byrnes. The administration, with the president and Byrnes, still wanted their country to be friends toward its wartime ally. Russia experts seemed to be with Churchill and ahead of others. Russia would not leave Iranian soil, and Turkey seemed a ripe plum for the Soviets to pick. Sensing the West's alertness, however, Russia backed off.

The president sent to the Mediterranean a navy flotilla, significantly built around the new aircraft carrier USS *Franklin D. Roosevelt,* to protect the West's interests and Turkey. Thus may have begun Truman's policy of containment of the Soviets. As Forrestal noted in his diary, Truman told his advisers, "We might as well find out whether the Russians were bent on world conquest now as in five or ten years." Truman's top policy makers understood that America's awakening to Soviet pretensions could mean war. Did the president understand? Yes.

While these tensions were almost at a boiling point, a plan to put atomic weapons under international control was dead at the White House. There was little enthusiasm to place atomic weapons, or fuel, under international control. A subsequent, similar, idea—the Baruch Plan—met the same fate. Russia was not interested in any international hold on atomic bombs and bomb-making. It was building its own atomic bomb and did not want to give that up. In his *Memoirs,* Truman wrote: "We should not under any circumstances throw away our gun until we are sure the rest of the world can't arm against us." At one point, Oppenheimer visited Truman and in agony said that he, Oppenheimer, had "blood on his hands." Truman replied that the blood was on his own hands. Truman, and not Oppenheimer, had ordered the atomic bomb to be used to end the war. The president thought the scientist a "crybaby."

It is hard to say whether it was about this time that the Cold War began, but it comes close. At this time, both the Soviet Union and Britain asked the United States for big loans. Britain was to get one but the Soviets did not. In Europe, cooperation between the US and the USSR was breaking down over German currency. Money had to be printed for the reorganizing, defeated nation, and how its value was to be adjusted to other countries' currencies was debated. The question of agricultural exports was another bone of contention: Germans were starving, so how could they export much grain (also to a starving Russia)? And then there was the question of reparations—the Soviets wanted German industrial machinery and every possible asset to assist their own renovation. The Western allies decided that Germany had to be rebuilt as a bulwark against Russian truculence. Thus, the United States and Britain merged their zones of occupation in Germany, to gain greater leverage in a rising battle for strength against Soviet imperialism. It was another step in the march toward coldness between the West and Russia.

All this was taking place without any public statement of a changed policy on the part of the Western Allies until September, when Byrnes revealed that US policy was to rebuild Germany toward Western values. Two famous memos by Kennan helped inform Truman and policy makers of Russian intentions, indeed intentions that went back centuries, despite a change in government from Tsar-based despotism to Soviet dictatorship. One, from 1946, came to be called the Long Telegram, and the other, from 1947, enunciated the policy of containment. A final sentence of a Kennan report, as recounted by Truman's aide Clark Clifford, was hair-raising: "The United States must be prepared to wage atomic and biological warfare if necessary." From all we know of Truman's values and lessons learned by war, this coda could not easily be accepted by him. His aversion to using atomic weapons again was strong, and biological warfare off his chart. There were divisions in Truman's cadre of advisers, but he remained a centrist, listening to both sides, but knowing that he was dealing with no Pendergast in Stalin. The Soviet leader was not a give-and-take conciliator, not a political boss, but a scheming dictator.

The containment policy—of aid and peaceful negotiations—was being militarized in policy makers' minds, however. Friendship with the Soviets appeared a doomed proposition. All agreed but Henry Wallace, the Secretary of Commerce, who was the most desirous of keeping Russian friendship. He wrote a speech for a big New York rally, which he showed Truman, who seemed to assent to it. Whether he actually did became a great dispute. Wallace challenged the administration's policy toward Russia. He endorsed the Soviet sphere of influence in Europe and favored economic aid to the USSR. Byrnes was furious with Wallace's break with administration policy. Truman asked Wallace to resign. His diary records that he saw Wallace and his backers as "a sabotage front for Uncle Joe Stalin." Harriman replaced Wallace as Secretary of Commerce. There was never a chance that Truman was preparing to go to war with Russia, to engage in another world war. The president reminded historians that he was like the Old Europeans, who looked askance as the Russians, under the Romanovs, over centuries, continually expanded their empire. European interventions were futile then, and without declaring another war, would be futile now. Truman remained in the middle of the furious battle among his advisers because there were still peace treaties to be signed, and he was even thinking about a loan to Russia to draw it into conciliation.

Truman had a commendable record as a wartime leader, as commander in chief, as required by the Constitution. Postwar, when he had to preside over a domestic economy, he was less a leader than befuddled. He was often angry over events unfolding, full of blame, and often rudderless. He thought of himself as a good New Dealer, but how could that program translate to the peacetime economy, with its pent-up consumer desires, demands for more food worldwide, reconversion to peacetime industry, labor's demands for wage hikes, industry's wish for higher prices, the elimination, or not, of price controls, and tax reconsiderations. He faced a veritable storm of wind, rain, hail, snow, brickbats, and scorn. Everyone wanted his own solution. He needed a coherent program. He had none. The 1946 congressional elections loomed as his greatest problem, and he lost the battle. House Republicans swept in, 246–188 (with the American Labor Party getting one seat). The Senate was Republican, 51–45. Republicans had found a winning slogan for voters: "Had Enough?" Other effective slogans were: "To Err Is Truman" and "Two Families in Every Garage." Resemblances to what Democrats had used to malign Hoover in 1932 were everywhere. It was devastating. When he returned from voting in Missouri, the only reception he got at Union Station was from the sympathetic acting Secretary of State, Dean Acheson. Truman blustered to Bess in a letter: "I'm doing as I

damn please for the next two years and to hell with all of them."
He told a Gridiron dinner: "Sherman was wrong. . . . I find peace
is hell." His temper was out of control, as he faced almost insu-
perable problems. And he lacked Roosevelt's soothing gift in
talking to the people, letting some things take care of themselves, allowing all to think he was on their side, and making
decisions only when necessary, after consulting experts.

What had gone wrong from the end of the war until the end
of 1946? Churchill, another great wartime leader, had already
been repudiated by the voters over his domestic program. Now
it was Truman's turn to face the nation. On September 6, 1945,
he had sent a message to Congress, a largely uninspiring document in two parts. The first part spelled out getting the soldiers
home, a resumption of consumer product manufacture, a continuing of some wartime controls. The second part was a grab
bag of old ideas from the 1930s and new programs. It included
a national health insurance plan, a program for education, and
a reform of Social Security. That second part was an imaginative
expansion of the New Deal. Then there were suggestions for
extended unemployment benefits, a Fair Employment Practices
Act, a large housing program, better veterans' benefits, and a
Lend Lease settlement. A far-sighted addition was the establishment of a National Science Foundation. The president continued with a plan for public works and regional development
of natural resources. It was a document that Congress could
dine out on for a decade, and the longest document aimed at
Congress since the irrepressible Teddy Roosevelt was president.
Congress chose not to bite. It was a more conservative body

after the 1946 elections, the people were tired of strenuous effort, and there was a yearning for a known stability.

A few things were accomplished. On the question of full and fair employment, something civil rights advocates wanted, Truman got a weak-as-water bill. A new Council of Economic Advisers was set up, but it became a paper organization. There was a worldwide famine, and Truman made his response a part of his agricultural program, got help from Herbert Hoover, who had done a great job feeding Europe after World War I, and farmers worked with him. The program raised prices at home but seemed the right thing to do. A balance had to be sought between raising wheat for food or for beef cattle: a seesaw emerged and was not resolved for months.

A great turmoil after the war was between unions wanting higher wages and manufacturers wanting higher prices and restrained wages. Truman thought labor wanted too much and was furious. He seized one industry after another to end strikes—steel, coal mines, tugboats, railways. His tough language was recorded in his *Memoirs*. He wrote that he told two union leaders: "You are not going to tie up the country. If this is the way you want it, we'll stop you." A million people were on strike, and the president was besieged. Once more, he was tough in his *Memoirs,* about measures he took and some he fantasized about. He mentioned declaring an emergency and calling out the troops. He mused about court-martialing leaders and shooting one particular labor nemesis of his. Had the president lost his rationality? He asked Congress to draft strikers. It did not. The president realized that the forces unleashed by peace were beyond his control, though he managed to veto an anti-labor bill. He was unsteady, bobbing and weaving; he had not acquired the political knack to lead the Congress or people. These were not his finest months. What to blame? A Washington journalist later laid out the possibilities: "Ill luck, ill preparation, inexperience, incompetence, and the dislocations of the war."

One of the most challenging issues for Truman, nestled among domestic problems, was the question of nuclear control. He asked Congress for a United States Atomic Energy Commission. He wanted to head it; others thought it ought to be led by the military. The War Department drafted the document and privileged itself. After waffling, Truman favored another bill with a strong civilian leadership. He appointed as the first chairman an excellent choice, David Lilienthal, who had headed up the successful Tennessee Valley Authority (TVA). The president received help from the Senate, at last. An ancillary desire of Truman's was universal military training, an American ideal going back to the Revolution, the citizen soldier. He always idealized the role the National Guard played in World War I and thought less of the regular army, so steeped in tradition and rules, it had little or no initiative in war. The idea went nowhere. Minute Men, yes, but they were farmers with guns. Taking sons into military service seemed a foreign concept, and foreign countries with standing militaries seemed to start wars.

Truman was the man in the arena, sooty, scarred, dazed. He felt the public lacked confidence in him. He saw himself as a heroic figure and the people as selfish.

He was exhausted and claimed that he was reading 30,000 words of memos per night. (One should recall how Truman's successor, Dwight Eisenhower, met this kind of deluge; he ordered his staff to prepare memos of only one page for him to read.) Truman wrote to his mother: "The pressure here is becoming so great I hardly get my meals in, let alone what I want to do." His relations with his beloved Bess, at home in Independence, also were strained, a situation unlike any he had ever experienced. He could not get home for the Christmas holidays, as she expected, until Christmas Eve, flying, against advice, through a terrible snowstorm. On returning to Washington, he wrote her a letter on December 28, in response to her cold reception. Like so many angry missives, however, he never sent it. It showed how low his emotional strength had dipped: "You can never appreciate what it means to come home as I did the other evening after doing at least one hundred things I didn't want to do and have the only person in the world whose approval and good opinion I value look at me like I'm something the cat dragged in and tell me I've come in at last because I couldn't find any reason to stay away."

Truman always needed Bess and her love to stabilize his emotions, but she still spent too much time with her mother in the old mansion in Independence, which she preferred to the White House. A bright spot in family life the next year was that his brother Vivian rebought the Truman homestead for their mother. Sadly, it was too late for her because she was too ill to move. Still, the act was kind and closed the circle of family affection. Truman was making the most money he ever had, with a salary of $75,000 a year, a great success in the extended family, which must have pleased him, although his unforgiving mother-in-law still called him Mr. Truman, even when he was president. The money surely became an element, very minor, to be sure, for him to hang onto the presidency. He had no other resources, and there was no pension for presidents.

Back to work, Truman planned an angry message to Americans: "If you people insist on following Mammon instead of Almighty God—your President cannot stop you all by myself." Strained and upset, he addressed the American people, but in a softer version than he had planned. And he wrote a memo to himself about American greed, after winning a great war victory, and the fair or foul means that special interests used to grab what they could. He was surrounded by "demagogues," "chiselers," the "jealous." Walter Lippmann, the great journalist, was more than disappointed by Truman's performance. He called the men about Truman "blunt trash." They did "not have the brains, and practicality, none of the wisdom from experience and education to help the President." This criticism came even though Truman had already begun replacing cabinet men with good appointments: Robert Patterson for Stimson, and Fred Vinson for Henry Morgenthau as Secretary of the Treasury. (The latter, it should be noted, Truman did not like, calling him a "nut" and a "blockhead" who "did not know shit from apple butter.") General Marshall was slated to replace Byrnes. Senator J. William Fulbright, a baron in that august body, thought Truman was such a failure he ought to appoint a vice president to take over and resign. Truman's acid response was to call the man from Arkansas Senator Half Bright.

On the positive side of the Truman ledger for these trying months were that there was no depression, the reconversion and recovery to peacetime work were going fairly well, money was cheap. He set up the CIA. And a foreign policy was taking shape that would guide future years. Basically, communism was to be contained wherever it poked its head out and whenever it threatened nations. It was a daunting commitment, world-wide, but popular in Congress and with the American people. Then, too, the Atomic Energy Act of 1946, with civilian control, not military, was a victory. When union leader John L. Lewis called a coal strike, almost as a bookend to balance the bad with the good, Truman bemoaned in a letter to a former ambassador: "It is difficult for me to understand why the necessity for two such men as [Soviet foreign minister V. M.] Molotov and John Lewis on earth at the same time as principal contenders for top rating as walking images of Satan."

In early 1946, Truman got a loan to Great Britain for $3.75 billion at 2 percent interest, but there were strings attached. The Imperial Preference, a tariff arrangement that favored countries within the British Empire, was abolished, and the pound sterling equivalence with the dollar was reset. The Soviets got nothing. Later, the president claimed offshore oil for the federal government, and not states, surely an enormous victory for the American people over grasping states. However, the whole question of oil and Truman's appointments on natural resources disagreed with what Secretary of Interior Harold Ickes, a New Deal holdover of great competence and irascibility, expected. Events boiled up over differences on how to protect the nation's natural resources until Ickes resigned. He characterized Truman as "neither an absolute monarch nor a descendant of a putative Sun Goddess." Truman pushed on and recommended statehood for Alaska and Hawaii. Incredibly, he projected a surplus for 1947.

Truman had just about concluded, as noted in his diary on September 26, 1946, that "the human animal and his emotions change not from age to age. He must change now or he faces absolute and complete destruction and maybe the insect age or an atmosphereless planet will succeed him." He had in mind the late dark and difficult happenings on the domestic scene, as well as in the world. It was a bleak outlook. Uncle Sam's whiskers had been twisted, getting to this point. It is sometimes written that Truman's record up to this point was a remarkable achievement. If so, it was based on his wartime and foreign policy decisions. Domestically, his record was spotty. Perhaps it could not be otherwise. If England could throw out the great Churchill, could Truman not be far behind?

Truman remained in a dark mood, when he wrote to his daughter about the presidency, which "no man in his right mind" would want. To succeed, he wrote, a president had to be a "liar, double-crosser" combining traits and talents of the ruthless Machiavelli, Talleyrand, Louis XI of France, and Cesare Borgia.

That summer Margaret and Bess went home to Independence; Truman sent Vinson to the Supreme Court and John Snyder became Secretary of the Treasury. Truman was ill with stomach pains and nerves. His body remembered how to respond when under deep stress. His approval rating dropped to

32 percent. He thought he heard or saw the ghost of Lincoln stalking the White House. He needed a vacation.

Nineteen forty-seven was a turning point in Truman's presidency. The trajectory turned upward, with foreign policy projected forward and domestic concerns taking a back seat. But while there would be great victories, the Republicans tarred policy makers and the president himself with a reddish taint and almost turned victories into defeats or, at least, put them in shadow. The bright sun of later years reveals how significant the charges were. The new Congress now contained Richard Nixon and Henry Cabot Lodge in the Senate and John F. Kennedy in the House. Senator Robert Taft of Ohio, son of a president, astute, cold, and calculating, who wanted to be president someday, was the natural leader in the Congress and implacably hostile to Truman in foreign policy. He was isolationist, although somewhat amenable to social programs when they touched veterans' needs. The Congress immediately revealed that it was hostile to anything smacking of the New Deal. It was intent on stopping communism, abroad and at home.

Truman's Key West respite was just what he needed, for he returned to Washington as a strong political soldier. Frank McNaughton of *Time* recorded the most interesting view of the president as he faced this new, more conservative Congress. Truman was now "confident, assured . . . compared with the scared little man who stepped shaky into Roosevelt's large shoes." Truman was rebuilding his staff with some remarkable men to guide him. It could almost be said that he was as good as his staff was. His first group of advisers had been as inexperienced as he was, in giving advice or knowing who to turn to. Now Truman added men to his staff like Clark Clifford, a political wizard, as well as the knowledgeable James Rowe, among others. And there would be changes in the cabinet, both kitchen and formal. Simultaneously, it was helpful that the economy was bouncing back and there was almost full employment. Times were good; the pent-up demand for consumer goods was being met.

Truman was confident, as reflected in his diary, and made several significant decisions. He decided to counter Soviet expansion, most immediately to threats against Greece and Turkey, with economic and military assistance. The policy was soon dubbed the Truman Doctrine: he would assist any nation under threat by the Soviets. The Senate agreed, and he won this first struggle by a three-to-one margin in both houses of Congress. If there were early nails sealing the coffin of the Cold War, this was the last one. These endangered nations would soon puncture Soviet dreams. It's not that all congressmen were cooperating in Truman's endeavors, for Truman wrote to his family on February 17 that, while entertaining them at the White House, as was the custom, "there were a half dozen" he "would rather have punched in the nose." Continuing along this fighting line, he wrote, again, on March 28: "Woodrow Wilson said that most members of Congress just had a knot on their shoulders to keep their bodies from unraveling."

Truman drove himself to put meat on the bones of the Truman Doctrine. He secured the Rio Treaty of twenty-one countries in the Western hemisphere that pledged joint action to address aggression, either from the outside, or against each other. Latin America was safe from communism's intrusion, as indeed the earlier Monroe Doctrine had warned Europe not to interfere in Latin American affairs, that triumph under Secretary of State John Quincy Adams. (Later, there would be NATO, SEATO, and the Baghdad Pact drawn along similar lines.) When Byrnes left office—he was too much of a lone ranger for Truman—the president appointed one of the nation's greatest war heroes, George C. Marshall, as Secretary of State. In this premier post the general soon made possible the well-financed program for a starving and devastated Europe that took his name, the Marshall Plan. Once again, a report by Herbert Hoover helped the bill in Congress. Marshall put George Kennan as head of the Policy Planning Staff with the admonition to think big. Acheson stayed on in his post as Undersecretary of State. The Ivy League elitist found Truman refreshing, after having himself been thought ordinary by Roosevelt, who was of the same heritage and so could condescend to others of his stripe. That Acheson soon left to make money in the law to support his family and enable him later to return to public life was not too great a blow because Robert Lovett took over. He was of equal social status to Acheson, and he was Harriman's business partner, wealthy, and a skilled political tactician. The snobby State Department accepted him.

Truman, a tight-fisted budget hawk, hoped to pay for the Marshall Plan by taking money from appropriations for defense and Asia. Marshall had recently gone to China to try to get the Nationalists under Chiang Kai-shek and the Communists to form a coalition government. He had not succeeded. The State

Department and Truman found Chiang one of the most corrupt leaders, more money lining the pockets of politicians and generals than meeting war needs; they saw no hope for success, no matter how much aid was promised. China fell to the Communists in 1949. With such a huge loss to the West's hopes for a free China, the defense budget Truman had intended to pare by one third or one quarter was doomed. The hot war was over, but the Cold War was getting colder. Truman was establishing himself as a strong president, with tight control over the military and foreign policy, but he did not foresee the rock-strewn path before him. Chiang fled to Formosa vowing to return to the mainland and set up a second faux China. He had powerful friends in the Congress and the country, while the Defense Department, under Forrestal, had ties to industry that President Eisenhower would later call a menacing military-industrial complex. The country was now overcommitted in the world, and defense money was not sufficient. Furthermore, relying on the atomic bomb for defense—Truman thought the US had about fourteen bombs—was not the bulwark needed. It was too devastating a response, if America's national interests were challenged. And preventive war was not on the table. There is no indication from Truman's records that he had changed his mind about never using the terror weapon again, if he could help it.

The Soviets, by their offensive actions, enabled Truman's containment and economic aid programs to get through Congress. Communists seized power in Czechoslovakia in 1948, a brave, small country that had tried to war against Hitler but was deceitfully given away in pieces in a Munich Pact between England and Germany, for "peace in our time." It was the last democracy in Eastern Europe. Truman got the military draft extended. Then Finland fell into the Soviet orbit. European nations organized a collective defense pact—Britain, France, Belgium, Luxembourg, the Netherlands. Italy beat back the Communist Party in elections, and Western nations began forming West Germany, uniting their zones. The Soviets began to harass Western traffic to Berlin. Congress passed a $6 billion foreign aid bill, most to go to the Marshall Plan, and the drumbeat of the Cold War got louder. Truman was more than elated by Congress's cooperation, and counted the containment of the Soviets and economic aid to the war-torn European nations as among his great achievements. But, at times, he lapsed into making sometimes puzzling, sometimes profane statements. At a dinner party, for example, he said that what he should have been was "a piano player in a whorehouse."

In the middle of the turbulent years of the 80th Congress, a new chapter was beginning in world history, needing its own bright spotlight. On May 14, 1948, at 6 PM, Israel declared itself a state. Truman immediately granted it de facto recognition. Less than two weeks later, he received a Torah from Chaim Weizmann, president of Israel. It was one of the few times Truman teared up. In return Truman relayed to him his decision to act positively for Israel. But it was not the end, but the beginning, of trouble for the president. He acted against the advice of the State Department, General Marshall, and Warren Austin, the head of the US delegation at the UN, and Britain. The UN had voted to partition Palestine into two states, with Jerusalem as a separate city, in November 1947. The Arab states had not accepted this. England held a mandate for Palestine, given to it after the Great War, but could not find a solution to the problem. When a trusteeship was proposed—that is, placing the country in the hands of a major power to rule it but also preparing it for independence—Austin approved without consulting Truman. The president thought the State Department had "cut his throat" by agreeing to this new arrangement. The officialdom at State was Arabist, and not pro-Israel. Truman was lambasted from all sides, especially from a segment of the New Deal coalition, the Jewish voters. Truman, a good historian, knew the new state had been promised to Jews by England, in 1917, in the Balfour Declaration, but England wanted to give up its mandate and let others decide Palestine's fate. Truman only wanted "to make the whole world safe for Jews," he recalled in his *Memoirs*. When he was told that a trusteeship might cost the UN 100,000 troops, almost half of them coming from the United States, which would be all of the nation's ground reserves, it was a blow to the trusteeship plan. Still, when it was the state of play, Truman backed Austin. It was an exasperating and humiliating moment for Truman, who recorded: "I surely wish God Almighty would give the Children of Israel an Isaiah, the Christians a St. Paul and the Sons of Ishmael a peep at the Golden Rule." When he was harassed, he blurted out: "If the Jews refuse to accept a truce on reasonable grounds they need not expect anything else from us." The end was war, as Syria and Lebanon crossed into what was now declared Israel, with

Iraq to follow. Five Arab nations, all Israel's neighbors, declared war on Israel, although not all invaded the fledgling state. In a bitter war, Israel won its independence.

Truman's decision was basically a moral one, a biblical promise to be fulfilled, but it became a political one, as Israel and the Middle East became a new problem area for decades. The United Kingdom and American Arabists in the State Department had more than morality and politics on their minds. The Arabs controlled immense oil fields, and oil fueled Britain's large navy, after it was retrofitted in 1902 and dreadnoughts were built, as well as Anglo-American cars, the military, and homes. Oil had been at the core of England's (and France's) broken promises to Arabs, who thought they had won their freedom on the battlefields of the Great War, only to be bitterly disappointed when a secret treaty of 1916, the Sykes-Picot Agreement, was made public. In that document England and France had agreed to form and parcel out Arab countries between themselves, which they proceeded to do, establishing the states then existing, with their almost nonsensical boundaries, breaking up tribes, and creating kingships. Truman's backdrop was not oil but Deuteronomy and its promises.

I t could be said that the 1946 elections forged the Republican Party as it is known today. Its centerpiece was the rolling back of the New Deal whenever and wherever possible. It aimed its first shot at labor. Truman was ambivalent, after suffering so many strikes after the war. Something had to be done, but what? In his State of the Union Address in January 1947 he opposed secondary boycotts and jurisdictional strikes, especially. Senator Taft and New Jersey Representative Fred Hartley put together a more extreme anti-labor bill—the Taft-Hartley bill. The president would be given injunctive power to put off strikes for eighty days, unions could not give to federal candidates for office, and the closed shop (where employers could hire only union members) was outlawed, among other measures. Truman vetoed the bill, and Congress overrode the veto, 331 to 83 and 68 to 25. As it turned out, the act did not prove as deleterious as predicted by New Dealers, and Truman found it useful. But the labor movement hated it, and they were a major part of the old New Deal coalition.

Inflation was another trouble for Truman, especially high food prices. Taft helped him out when he began his foot-in-mouth disease, saying that people ought to "eat less meat and less extravagantly." It was an eat-your-oatmeal statement, which caused a brouhaha. Truman's answer to the inflation problem was a return to controls, a non-starter.

Resourceful, Republicans grabbed onto a congeries of related issues that would cause much heartbreak and was to be political poison for the administration: alleged subversion in government; disloyalty to America; socialism, that is, the New Deal; the spread of communism from the Soviet Union to satellites; and totalitarianism, fascism, or any domestic measure of reform. By now, the Cold War raised fears, and a few espionage cases were blown out of proportion to blacken Democrats and Truman. The president had unwisely issued an executive order on March 21, 1947, extending a wartime Loyalty Program with a loyalty board to investigate the background of government employees for ties to subversive organizations, particularly the Communist Party. In Congress, the House Un-American Activities Committee (HUAC) was conducting hearings to ferret out communists in government, with little attention to due process or the protections of the Constitution. Truman received the HUAC report in October 1947. Why did he latch on to what became an hysterical phase in the country's history? (The Alien and Sedition Acts of the 1790s, which destroyed John Adams's presidency, were similarly disastrous.) Perhaps Truman was trying to steal the thunder of communist-chasing Republicans. Whatever. The outcome was that liberty was under threat by government snooping in all federal employees' lives. When the extreme consequences of his own action, now in peacetime, became obvious to Truman, he was outraged by the scope and depth of a host of investigations by Congress, seeing the "Gestapo" (his word) at work. As it turned out, among 2.5 million federal employees, only 400 to 1,200 were suspect. The loyalty order was allowing a cannon to fire, when a flyswatter would do. Truman was the responsible agent in the broad attack by congressional committees on civil liberties. Unconscionably, his approval rating shot up to 60 percent. When Democrats took over on Truman's coattails in his 1948 victory, all civil rights legislation was thwarted by the Southern wing of the party, in control of committees through the seniority system. Then, when the Korean War broke out in June 1950, Truman was consumed by it, and the work of the civil rights coalition was disrupted.

But to return to 1947 and 1948: although it was early, Truman and his staff began to think about the 1948 presidential election. The president needed to emboss his New Deal threads. His January 7, 1948 State of the Union Address was his broadest attempt to recapture the liberal agenda. Each cohort in the old New Deal coalition was to be courted in its geographical area: the West, reclamation and flood control; the eastern cities, labor benefits, higher minimum wage; the rural areas, agricultural supports; blacks, civil rights; Jews, support for Israel; Catholics, fighting godless Communism. There was a call for higher corporate taxes and a tax rebate for each taxpayer. Afterward, the president went on a veto binge: vetoes on a tax cut twice, a trade bill raising a tariff on wool, the removal of newspaper vendors from the social security system. The last, inscrutable. He asked for housing aid, assistance for education, national health insurance. James Reston of the *New York Times* was unimpressed: "Mr. Truman was long on rags and tatters and short on pattern. . . . He did not clarify the central issues but confused them. . . . He did not provide a priority list for the new year's problems but merely lumped them together."

Surprisingly for a former senator, Truman did not keep in touch with the Democratic leaders about his desires. He was leading without seeing whether any followers were behind him. Senator Barkley complained of "playing a night ball game. . . . I'm supposed to be the catcher and I should get signals. I am not only not getting the signals, but someone actually turns out the lights when the ball is tossed." Truman was more concerned with showing how he differed from Republicans than concili-

ating and wasting time with out-of-power Democratic leaders.
He needed the spotlight to himself. Rank-and-file Democrats
liked him. His Gallup poll rating in June was 48 percent, a good
number. He kept looking toward elements in the old New Deal
coalition. Blacks became important, and that meant attention
to civil rights. In June 1947, from the steps of the Lincoln Memorial, he had spoken to an audience of 10,000 attending the
annual convention of the National Association for the Advance-
ment of Colored People, the first president to address the organization. He enunciated the promise that the government
had to lead the way in establishing civil rights to *all,* including
good housing, medical care, economic entitlements, and protection against prejudice and discrimination. In October 1947
the Committee on Civil Rights, which he had appointed in
1946, published its proposals in a report, *To Secure These Rights.*
He had not always been interested in rights for the black population; rather he waffled because of his family's Southern roots,
but when a number of postwar outrages were perpetrated
against black veterans, he had blurted out: "My God! I had no
idea that it was as terrible as that! We've got to do something."

The proposals of Truman's Committee on Civil Rights were
more far reaching than his already known civil rights policy, as
it included anti-lynching laws, the end of the poll tax, voting
rights, desegregation of the armed services, a new division of
civil rights within the Justice Department, help in civil suits,
and the organization of the United States Commission on Civil
Rights. When Truman issued an executive order on December
5, 1946, creating the President's Committee on Civil Rights, it

was to protect the civil rights of the people of the United States. The committee's report, *To Secure These Rights,* was a bombshell in the South, which was a major source of Democratic votes, and even stirred up some white opposition in the rest of the country. After all, poor whites thought of themselves as having some status because they were historically socially above the blacks. Truman welcomed the report and sent up legislation in February 1948, in a ten-point program. Among his recommendations for action were anti-lynching and anti–poll tax laws, fair employment practices, the end of segregation in interstate transportation, and home rule and anti-discrimination in the District of Columbia, which was federally ruled. He did not address discrimination in education. Truman did not fight hard for his program, given the southern control of Congress. Then, too, the immediate reaction in the country was negative. The proposed laws were quickly deemed disastrous. It took almost a generation for a president to touch this subject again.

There were bets that Truman would not win the bid to run again for president. Even the *New York Times* held this position. Liberals didn't like him; some flirted with Eisenhower, until he took himself out of the Democratic column; some started a rump movement, Americans for Democratic Action (ADA), and some put themselves forth. Truman held firm, winning caucuses and primaries, had firm and powerful allies like Rayburn and Barkley, and tightened his control over the Democratic National Committee. He was, by now, a seasoned national politician, who knew what strings to pull. He continued his attacks on the 80th Congress, which was passing anti-

liberal legislation on social issues, sometimes over Truman vetoes. He asked the people in speeches to vote for a Congress
that favored the common people and not those who have all
the money. He was thought of as carrying Roosevelt's banner,
as he demanded that Congress pass his eight liberal measures
before them; only one of them did get through, that to help
farmers. True to form, Truman's mother-in-law was recorded
as saying to friends that it was a waste of time for Truman to
run against the Republican ticket. The *Chicago Tribune* called
the president a "nincompoop." The acerbic Clare Booth Luce
called him a "gone goose."

Democrats met the week of July 14 in Philadelphia. Truman
won the Democratic nomination for president on the first ballot, 947 and a half votes to 263, but the South walked out over
the civil rights plank and founded the States Rights Party, or
the Dixiecrat Party. Strom Thurmond of South Carolina
headed the ticket. Henry Wallace would also form the Progressive Party and lead the ticket. It was like old times, in the nineteenth century, with four parties vying for president. Truman
chose the garrulous but likeable Alben Barkley to run as vice
president. He was as careless in thinking about second place as
Roosevelt had been in 1944. In his acceptance speech, given at
two in the morning to desperately tired delegates, Truman challenged prosperous farmers and labor to dare not to vote for him,
after all he had done for them. Then he threw a grenade into
national politics, by announcing that he was going to call the
Congress into special session to get bills passed. He wanted his
adversaries in open daylight. He told his staff he would taunt

the Republicans: "Now you sons of bitches, come and do your God damnedest."

Truman hit all the old buttons in campaigning, despite the fact that the country had turned more conservative with the 1946 elections: economic controls, education aid, civil ethno-religious rights, national health insurance, a higher minimum wage, extended social security, liberalized immigration, publicly owned power. He attacked Republican stand-pattism and incompetence. Liberals were energized. *The New Republic* summed it up: "It was fun to see the scrappy little cuss come out of his corner fighting." Truman was fired up and told Barkley: "I'll mow 'em down. . . . I'll give 'em hell."

Republicans were also looking to the 1948 presidential election. The GOP contenders for president were Thomas E. Dewey, former gangbusting district attorney of New York County and current governor of New York, who had lost to Roosevelt in 1944; Senator Vandenberg; and Harold Stassen, former governor of Minnesota. They played on Democratic unhappiness with Truman, whose poll numbers were dropping, and Truman was eyeing Eisenhower as the Democratic candidate, though Eisenhower had already told him he was not interested. The president was a fighter, however, and had decided he would run for a term all his own.

Truman puzzled out what he needed to do to win. He clutched the New Deal label, but more was needed. He lacked Roosevelt's human touch. But to know Truman was to like him. He was able to get the very private Bess to agree to travel with him, and, of course, Margaret went along, as his first, devoted supporter. Beyond the happy family theme, Truman's handlers had to find a way to unleash him and get him out on the stump. Truman's plan was to board a train and hit every hamlet he could over many weeks. Speaking extemporaneously—although research notes were at the ready—was his forte. He was genial and warm in person-to-person encounters. His stories could be crafted, for he had been a farmer, a small businessman licked by inflation and recession, a local politician who built roads and infrastructure and gave jobs, a friend of labor, and an authentic cracker-barrel character with a fund of low, or common, jokes.

A luxurious train, the *Ferdinand Magellan,* was got up for extended trips by Truman and family by the Pullman Company. It was a veritable moving Little White House. The train was eighty-three feet long, the windows were three-inch-thick bulletproof glass, all cars were armor-plated on all sides, and it weighed 142.5 tons. It held a galley, a pantry, servants' quarters, an oak-paneled dining room (and conference room), a mahogany dining table and six matching chairs in gold and green damask. There were four staterooms—one for Harry, one for Bess, and two middle rooms—with a minute bath and shower for the Trumans. Fixtures were satin chrome. All was carpeted. An observation lounge with blue walls had brown chairs and sofa and velvet curtains. Finally, an observation deck and speakers allowed for speeches at the back of the train. The whole affair was air conditioned with ice. In its ambience it seemed to be America's own Orient Express, although we do not know whether the food and service were fit for kings and queens, pashas, and millionaires. Truman had first tried it out going to California for a special occasion and then made it his rolling White House in campaigning. Climbing aboard in the fall, Truman was off, with Bess and Margaret, and a working staff of seventeen across the country for weeks at a time. He wanted to greet the people and give them a chance to see him. (He received White House mail and Congressional bills every day.) He exhausted his entourage, but he seemed to gain confidence and strength from the exercise. He was a regular Antaeus. The crowds were huge everywhere he stopped, even during the night, and he sometimes appeared in pajamas, robe, and slippers, so as not to disappoint people. Bess disapproved. The buttoned-up and totally controlled Dewey would never be seen like that.

When Truman took the train into northern and western states, he made some errors, like calling Stalin "Uncle Joe." His staff pounced on him and gave him advice about what was a winning speech, and gave him better notes to study. It was Truman who decided, however, to keep mostly to domestic issues, and he hit on a winning strategy to attack not Dewey but the 80th Congress. It was a "do-nothing" or a "good-for-nothing" body. Tens of thousands heard this, as well as the influentials, who also showed up. His crowds lapped it up. Richard Rovere, the journalist, was impressed by the people's reaction to him and predicted they would give him anything he wanted but the presidency.

Returning to Washington after one long journey, Truman faced a major international crisis. After the war, Berlin had been divided into Allied and Soviet sectors, and the Soviets were now blocking the Allies from all rail, road, and canal access into the city. The Soviets were showing their displeasure toward recent, collective Allied actions and wanted to test the resolve of the Americans, the principal Western power, to stay in a city surrounded by Soviet troops in the Soviet sector of Germany. It was a daring venture, if not an invitation to war. Truman decided not to challenge the Soviets on the ground, but sent B-29 bombers to England and Germany—the Soviets did not know they were not carrying atomic bombs—and tasked planes to supply Berlin by air. The military asked for atomic weapons to threaten Russia, but Truman rejected their request, telling it: "This isn't a military weapon. It is used to wipe out women and children and unarmed people. . . . This is no time to be juggling an atom bomb around." Once more, he kept the atom bomb under civilian control, the president's, but the military disagreed. For them, the atomic bomb was always considered a military weapon, like the largest of bombs. It was a part of the American military arsenal in a war.

Truman's civil rights bill was deep-sixed. Americans for Democratic Action, the new liberal group swelled by old New Dealers, liberals, and academics, and Roosevelt's sons, began challenging the president. The participation of his predecessor's sons made Truman furious. He dressed the sons down by telling them that he had taken the job of vice president at their father's behest, and that's the thanks he was getting from his sons. Some machine politicians did not want Truman, only because they thought he could not win, and winning was everything, and the

South, a major part of the Democratic coalition, was wobbling. Eisenhower's name was raised again, and the general batted it down. Truman, who had once urged Eisenhower to run for president as a Democrat with his backing, now called the famous general a "shit-ass," according to Truman's assistant press secretary, Eben Ayres. The barnyard language was sliding too easily off Truman's tongue when he was tired and sore beset.

When Congress reconvened, Truman was busy with an executive order that expanded equal opportunity in the federal civil service and in the armed forces, the latter, an earth-shaking revolution. He got nothing positive from Congress, but a miserable record that he could exploit on the hustings.

Truman continued to campaign on domestic issues. The Republican Congress was twisting itself inside out on communism's presumed attempt to overthrow the government. When GOP members saw communists under every bed, Truman saw Republican demagoguery. In September he stopped in seventeen states and traveled 8,300 miles in northern and western states, giving dozens of short stump speeches. He blamed all the domestic ills of the country on the Republicans. He mixed his liberalism with, in the memorable words of journalist Robert Donovan, "sophistries, bunkum piled higher than haystacks, and demagoguery tooting merrily down the track." At one stop in Iowa, 80,000 farmers showed up. Truman told them the Republicans had stuck a pitchfork in their backs. They yelled back: "Give 'em hell, Harry!"

The big train took Truman to the Northeast and back to the Midwest in October; later, to Florida, Massachusetts, and Mis-

FIGURE 18   October 2, 1948, at Union Station in Washington, DC, President Truman returns from a whistle-stop tour during the presidential campaign, with his wife, Bess, and daughter, Margaret. *Credit:* National Park Service, Abbie Rowe, courtesy of the Harry S. Truman Library.

souri. Sometimes he took to the air on the presidential plane, dubbed the *Sacred Cow,* for faster service. Truman was running a marathon. No one could keep up with him.

Dewey, who had won the Republican nomination for president, said he would never get down in the gutter with his adversary. He mused: "Isn't it harder in politics to defeat a fool, than, say, an abler man?" Walter Lippmann despised Truman's gadding about the country instead of staying in Washington and working at the presidency. Truman would often make up to eleven speeches in a fifteen-hour day, pressing, always pressing, the attack on the Congress. He traveled hundreds of miles at a time. He invoked Lincoln, when appropriate, to aid his cause. Fifty journalists were asked in a poll who was going to win the presidency, and they all said Dewey. Truman's response to the journalists' prophecy was: "There isn't one of them has enough sense to pound sand in a rat hole." Still, Truman had to contend with the reality that major newspapers praised Dewey: *New York Times, Los Angeles Times, Washington Star, Kansas City Star, St. Louis Post-Dispatch, Wall Street Journal.* Truman never flagged and worked the crowds up to Election Day. Looking back on the time, it can be calculated that it was in the last two weeks of the campaign that Truman surged ahead of Dewey. It was unnoticed by pollsters because they had stopped their work, so sure they were about who would win. They missed the significance of the huge crowds in the Northeast rallying for Truman. They missed the significance of New York City marching 50,000 persons for Truman and a million watching the parade, in Dewey's bailiwick. At the end, Truman became savage in attacks on Dewey. Unwisely, he linked him to fascism. The president remained relentless, and, in speech after speech, he laid into his adversaries.

Dewey, on the other hand, although a truly competent man, was wooden, and barely campaigned. Why bother, when the election was a shoo-in for him? All the polls, the newspapers, reporters, pundits, and assorted people said so. Actress Ethel Barrymore captured Dewey for all time with a sentence, made popular when Teddy Roosevelt's daughter Alice Longworth, the great gossip of Washington, took it up: "Dewey was like the little man on the wedding cake." Meantime, Henry Wallace was going nowhere. Thurmond excited only a few states. Truman,

FIGURE 19 President Harry Truman with former St. Louis mayor Bernard
F. Dickmann, holding the *Chicago Daily Tribune* showing the headline
"Dewey Defeats Truman," November 5, 1948. They are in the St. Louis
train station. *Credit:* Harry S. Truman Library.

alone, had a viable vehicle to victory, a resuscitated New Deal.
He had introduced ill-fated bill after ill-fated bill, in his revival
attempt, and reminded the crowds of his loyalty to those ideals
and programs. He promised to continue the fight.

Truman flew home to vote. The last Gallup poll had given
Dewey 49.5 percent and Truman 44.5 percent of the vote. I recall
Dewey's family getting ready to occupy the White House, when
his boys were inviting friends at my college, Barnard, elite girls
from the East Side of Manhattan, to Washington. Truman, on
election eve, disappeared into a hotel. Again? Back in his Pick-
wickian mode, he ordered a meal and went to bed, suggesting

that he be awakened only if something happened. By 10:14 the next morning, Dewey had conceded. Truman's favorite moment was holding up the *Chicago Daily Tribune* with the banner headline "Dewey Defeats Truman." Congress went Democratic. Labor helped the win. His pro-Israel stance cemented the Jewish vote for him. Rural areas were alight; farmer Truman got the farm vote. He took California and four southern states. All told, he carried twenty-eight states, with 303 electoral votes to Dewey's 189. In the popular vote, he took 24,105,812 votes to Dewey's 21,970,065; it was Truman 49.6 percent, Dewey 45.1, and Thurmond 2.4. Truman had pulled off the greatest electoral upset in American history. He had won as a man and not as a politician. He was the nation's reborn citizen soldier. The uptight Dewey, totally flummoxed, lost his temper on hearing his dismal results: "The son of a bitch won."

When Truman's train reached Union Station in Washington, 750,000 people greeted the hero. A band played "I'm Just Wild About Harry."

CHAPTER 7

KOREA AND THE FAIR DEAL

Truman's win was the most astounding political upset in all of American history. It was stunning beyond words to those who lived by words, to politicians, who worked for the best, but often were desperately pessimistic, to journalists, who always thought they knew more than the people. Truman was finally dubbed a man of the people, and he really was, unlike the often-cited Andrew Jackson, who owned a rich plantation in Tennessee with slaves. In anticipation of a Republican president, the first since Hoover, the Congress had appropriated $80,000 to celebrate the inauguration and had raised the president's salary to $100,000, with a tax-free expense account of $50,000. Truman was ecstatic and spent every dollar on the celebration, the gaudiest since before the war and depression, and relished the new money for his family. Blair House was comfortable and like a home, although Bess was warned that there were rats in the basement. According to gossiping servants, the very happy couple, Bess and Harry, were intimate in the president's bedroom, breaking the bed. The White House itself was scheduled to be reconditioned, from stem to stern, as ceilings were falling down, and the structure cracking. The president had an approval rating of 69 percent.

Truman's nickname now slid beyond Captain Harry, which his closest army buddies, even those who followed him into the White House, always called him, to Citizen Harry, the common man's president. He had a few months to rethink and reorganize his administration for this term in office that he had earned and had not been handed. He was as energetic as Theodore Roosevelt, whom he knew all about, when he won his own term. He gave his State of the Union Address in January 1949, as required by the Constitution and as his term was ending, and then planned for his Inaugural Address. In it, he highlighted accomplishments of the recent past, such as a continuation of the Marshall Plan and support to the UN, and then described a new treaty that would lead a few months later to the creation of the North Atlantic Treaty Organization, NATO. Then came the surprise, a program to assist third-world countries, which was later named the Point Four Program. The nation was prosperous, and Congress would approve the program the next year. The *New York Times*, the paper of national record, cited the inaugural address as one that greats like Lincoln, Theodore and Franklin Roosevelt, and Wilson would have commended.

The first few months of Truman's own term were somewhat tranquil. The Berlin blockade failed, Germany became a republic, again, after the more than disastrous epoch of Hitler's reign, and NATO was approved by Congress. The last was a collective security alliance of the wartime Allies pledged to protect themselves against enemies. These events were high achievements for the Truman presidency and burnished his reputation for significant successes in diplomacy. Europe was the epicenter of civilization, still, at the time, and its resuscitation, based on the highest of cultural achievements—of Bach and Galileo and Shakespeare—was epoch-making.

The Truman administration was, as ever, changing with the times. An ill Forrestal resigned as Secretary of Defense (and later committed suicide, to everyone's horror) and was replaced by Louis Johnson, a blustery persona who soon got into trouble. Then Tom Clark, a mediocre attorney general, was put on the Supreme Court, another mistake, it turned out. The unknown Howard McGrath replaced him. Truman's doctor found the president so fit he was called an "iron man." Success agreed with him. But Truman's euphoria was leading him astray.

Events soon turned into nightmares. As China fell to communism, a Red Scare arose in the country, aided and abetted by Senator Joseph McCarthy of Wisconsin and the new senator from California, Richard Nixon. Alger Hiss, a well-known State Department official, and friend of Dean Acheson, was called a spy for Russia. Acheson would not turn his back on him. Sensational trials ensued, but Hiss was found guilty only of perjury and was sent to jail. (Only much later, it was clear, with new evidence, that he had, indeed, been a spy.) China's fall to Mao Zedong was more serious, as $2 billion had been given to Chiang Kai-shek to bolster his government, which too many members

of Congress would not believe was corrupt and lacked leadership. The China lobby was strong and vocal, and the cry that
Truman lost China hurt bipartisan foreign policy. Negative happenings piled on. Truman's military aide Harry Vaughan and
others were accused of influence peddling in dispensing military contracts. Vaughan had also stupidly distributed food freez-
ers—a commodity hard to get, as yet—to friends, including
Bess, who returned hers. The Santa Claus was never charged
with a crime, but his inscrutable actions and lack of ethical behavior tarnished the new administration. Truman's loyalty to
his old friends had gone too far. Vaughan was never smart
enough to be in any high position, and certainly not in the
White House. He was a drinking and poker-playing old-soldier
buddy of the president, who was often lonely in the White
House without his family, and he had risen above the buffoon
state. Truman's only balance to these negative events was his
appointment of the elegant, returning Dean Acheson to be Secretary of State. In 1949, Russia detonated its first atomic bomb,
earlier by years than America's scientists had predicted. The appointment of Acheson, viewed by the Washington establishment as a tough and wise man of impeccable intellect, had not
come too soon. England's ambassador to the United States, the
likeable Oliver Franks, called Acheson a "blade of steel."

How the administration would face forthcoming, and ultimate, atomic parity with the Soviets became a more than burning issue within Truman's group of advisers. The quick answer
given to Truman by one body of atomic scientists was to build
the ultimate weapon, a hydrogen bomb, an H-bomb, more dev-

astating than anything yet conceived by man. It would have ten times the power of the atomic bombs used on Japan. It would put the United States back in the lead. How could Truman not build it, given the Soviets' truculent behavior? In his own mind, he decided to build it, even as his advisers were divided on the issue. Scientists like James Bryant Conant and Robert Oppenheimer opposed building it. Lewis Strauss of the Atomic Energy Commission and the physicist Edward Teller favored its development. At the time, Truman wrote to his family, without specifics, that he had succeeded in getting himself into more trouble than Pandora ever let loose in the world. He had already taken a rest in his Key West lair, but, once more, he needed a vacation. His headaches and other troubles returned, Bess worried about his stress, and off he went, again, to Florida. Maybe he was an iron man, but not a man of steel.

Truman's hectic life continued into 1950. He told Bess that he would not run for president in 1952 and left a private memo to that effect. A particularly important sentence in it was: "There is a lure in power. It can get into a man's blood just as gambling and lust for money have been known to do." Another big moment was when he was presented with a secret report intended to assess the nation's military strength, whose prime writer was Paul Nitze, never one to think the nation was truly prepared to defend itself in an uncertain world. On April 25 the National Security Council discussed it and was undoubtedly startled to learn that "containment" meant "bluff," nuclear weapons were not effective preventions, and the Soviets would catch up with the United States in nuclear capacity in 1954. The report called for a massive peacetime military buildup—later assessed as costing between $40 and $60 billion. It was a hot war, not a Cold War, report, which would become the defining document about America's gigantic military buildup under future presidents. Acheson viewed it as a "bludgeon," an unexpected weapon on policy makers by the military against a State Department engaged in peacemaking, its natural activity. Truman put the report in a drawer. He needed more information. He would not be rushed to judgment.

The heavens opened up on Truman on June 24, 1950, almost as angrily as when he had assumed office unexpectedly. While he was on a short visit home, Acheson phoned to inform him that communist North Korea was poised to invade South Korea, according to secret intelligence. In peace negotiations after the Second World War, Korea had been divided, the North communist (the Democratic People's Republic of Korea, or DPRK) and the South democratic (the Republic of Korea, or ROK), with the 38th parallel separating the two countries. When Acheson received the astounding news of the North Korean invasion, on his own he had called the secretary general of the United Nations to ask for a meeting of the Security Council, the executive body of the organization, before calling Truman. The president wanted to fly back to Washington immediately, but Acheson told him to get a good night's sleep and return to Washington the next day. At this point, Acheson was leading the president in this great epoch of tribulation and tragedy. Margaret Truman later wrote in her biography of her father that she knew he feared that this war-like incident was the opening of

World War III. Another call from Acheson told Truman that the invasion was not a feint, with other purposes, perhaps by other powers, but an "all-out offensive." Bess was tremulous, as emotionally upset as she was when Harry was sworn into office. Truman was furious: "By God, I am going to let them have it," he exclaimed when on the returning plane. He later wrote about his thinking: "When democracies failed to act, it encouraged aggressors." He did not think the invasion could go "unchallenged." American soldiers had already left Korea, where they were occupiers. Interestingly, Acheson had not considered Korea an area inside America's defense perimeter, and said so in a public speech. Yet here he was all stiff-backed over the invasion of a seemingly peripheral country. That was a true surprise. What was going on? The Security Council voted, 9–0, for a resolution calling for the end of hostilities and a withdrawal of forces to the 38th parallel.

Arriving back in Washington, Truman met with his advisers and Dean Rusk, who was in charge of Far Eastern Affairs in the State Department. Rusk gauged that a communist Korea—assuming that the better-prepared country, militarily, would overrun South Korea—was imperiling Japan. This mild-mannered man and Acheson, and others, all seemed gung-ho for war. A few wanted to draw the line, at this place, at this time, against communist aggression. Containment did not work, as all assumed that the USSR was behind the attack. (The Soviet ambassador on the Security Council had absented himself on the UN vote, having walked out earlier on another issue. He could have vetoed action, and did not. Later secret documents from

Soviet archives show that North Korea had decided months before June 1950 to invade the South.) Truman was being pulled
into a tightening circle for war. He saw the United States with
the "stronger hand." Military leaders thought that the navy and
air force could defeat the North Koreans. The army did not
want boots on the ground. Truman worried about Soviet ship
strength in Asia and what else the USSR might be contemplat-
ing. Later, he recorded how unanimous his advisers were about
meeting the aggression. Also later, Acheson wrote that this was
the "worst possible location to fight." To fight communism, that
is. Hindsight will not, perhaps ever, soften the reputation of
those who were so eager to send American soldiers to fight,
once more, on Asian soil, a vast not well-understood continent.
This would be first blood in the postwar world, but would not
be the last, as history would show about fighting on the Asian
continent. War in Vietnam, another country divided by treaty
between a communist north and a democratic south, was to
come. No lesson was learned from Korea. But this gets us beyond the Truman story, which is the opening gunshot of the
active militarization of the containment policy and the intro-
duction of the domino theory of countries falling, one after another, to communism if not stopped.

Truman's first act was to assist South Korea with arms and
supplies, to be funneled through General MacArthur in Japan.
Then American civilians were ordered to leave Korea, and the
Seventh Fleet was sent to guard the Formosa Strait. An interesting sidelight—to be recalled later—was that this early in the
epic to come, Secretary of Defense Johnson wanted instruc-

tions to MacArthur to be "detailed" with the general being allowed little "discretion." Truman thought he himself was acting
on behalf of the UN, most of all, as he never ceased to regret
that the League of Nations had failed in its duty to stop aggression by Hitler. MacArthur wired that the South Koreans were
about to collapse. Truman called another meeting of his war
cabinet. American naval and air support would now assist the
South Koreans, and the UN would be asked to back such activity. The president sent more troops to the Philippines and to
Indochina. But Truman told his war team: "I do not want to go
to war." Truman was more than cognizant that it was only five
years since the horrible World War II had ended with its great
carnage and the killing of innocents.

Why did Korea loom so large, all of a sudden, on the American horizon? A little background regarding Korea and the
United States is helpful here. The United States had a treaty
with Korea in effect since 1882—an unequal commercial document, as were all such treaties the West had with Asian nations. Korea was an ancient, unitary civilization, which became
a Japanese protectorate in 1905 and a colony in 1910. Theodore
Roosevelt, in thrall of Japanese power and Westernization, approved of Japanese actions. Japan had won a war against China
and then Russia and was determined to be the latest imperial
power in a world witnessing the seizure of countries in an imperial binge. After World War II, Truman approved an occupation policy and then midwifed the Republic of Korea in 1948.
Koreans were a contentious people after that, with Americans
trying to patch things up for them, but the war became a spear

into Truman's heart. It was never a popular war and dropped Truman's approval rating to 23 percent.

The Korean People's Army (KPA), in the North, was large: 74,370 strong, plus 20,000 border police. Twenty thousand troops were stationed in the far interior. The Republic of Korea Army (ROKA), the South, had 87,500 soldiers, with 35,000 at the 38th parallel and 35,000 a day's march away. The northern army, however, appeared to be superior in training and materiel.

On June 27, the ROK government fled south of the capital, Seoul, and the army followed. Seoul was taken by 37,000 northern troops, which, however, had lost half its army in the fighting. It was the utter collapse of the South that pushed the US into war. Acheson continued to dominate the conversation in committees, both military and State Department, and Truman listened. On June 27, the UN asked the US to intervene. On June 30, Truman made the momentous decision to send American ground forces, without consulting the Joint Chiefs of Staff, who he knew were opposed. At the time, the US had more than 668,000 men under arms. At first, MacArthur was cocky: "I can handle it with one arm tied behind my back." He asked for 30,000 troops, three tank battalions, and artillery. Soon, he asked for twice the number, or eight divisions. This was becoming serious war.

The Communists fielded 70,000 troops, the UN forces 92,000, with 47,000 being Americans. Almost immediately, retreat was the name of the game for the UN troops. South Koreans and Americans organized a defensive perimeter in the southeast, around Pusan, against 98,000 North Koreans. By

September, MacArthur had most of the fighting Americans he had asked for—83,000 Americans, plus 57,000 South Koreans and some British forces that had joined the UN mission. He had control of the air and five times the number of tanks the North had, and superior artillery. Two weeks of heavy fighting found the UN forces holding. By September 15, American casualties were 20,000 fallen, with 4,280 dead. MacArthur then made one of his brilliant strategic moves, counterattacking with a landing at Inchon, near Seoul. His troops were now behind the communists, catching them between UN forces. The landing became one of the classic battles of history and a turning point. There were 270 ships, and 80,000 marines hit the beach. Seoul fell to them. The North retreated, and MacArthur crossed the 38th parallel with his victorious men. The northern army retreated to the Yalu River, ever drawing MacArthur's forces northward. The North Koreans implored the Chinese to help them in this "planned withdrawal," to the Yalu, the South Koreans later claimed.

The North Koreans were not prepared for such a large American fighting force. They had thought they could end the war in a month. MacArthur's strategy left them reeling, although many officers and soon-to-be guerrilla forces escaped to the mountains. The toll was now 111,000 South Koreans killed, 106,000 wounded, and 57,000 missing. American casualties included 6,954 dead, 13,659 wounded, and 3,877 missing in action. (Some are still unaccounted for, and human remains are still being found, even today.) Probably the North Koreans lost 50,000 men. Truman could have ended the war at this point, with a great victory over communist aggression and kudos for the militarily defined containment policy. But he did not.

The administration decided that it would go for broke and roll back communist aggression, with Acheson leading the war pack. MacArthur was given permission to have the UN army invade the North, if no Soviet or Chinese threats were evident. In September and October the CIA and all other American intelligence reports were that the Chinese would not enter the war. The Joint Chiefs of Staff, with the approval of Acheson, Marshall (who became defense secretary in September 1950), and Truman, instructed MacArthur to destroy the North Korean army but not to cross international borders or attack Manchuria, or include actions against the USSR. With this directive, one must ask if Marshall was too old and tired to think and plan coherently. At yet another critical juncture in the nation's history, did the country have yet another old man at the defense helm who was not up to the job, Stimson coming to mind earlier? And Acheson wanted to prove that Western countries could assist others in danger across oceans. MacArthur relayed to the military back home that he considered all of Korea open for military operations. Truman thought he was only committing himself to the destruction of the North Korean army. After all, as he knew from his army experience, the German army fell apart after being driven back across the Rhine River. All along, it was never contemplated that when history repeats itself it might be not as reality but as farce.

Contradicting all intelligence reports, the Chinese decided to intervene and told the Soviets beforehand, we now know.

FIGURE 20 President Harry S. Truman and General Douglas MacArthur during the Wake Island Conference, October 15, 1950. *Credit:* Department of State, courtesy of the Harry S. Truman Library.

Truman had made a momentous decision when UN troops had crossed the 38th parallel. But things were now taking a perilous turn. He decided to fly to Wake Island, rather than recall MacArthur home, to confer, and took seventeen advisers, Acheson not among them as the secretary thought it a bad idea to talk with MacArthur. Truman wrote to his cousin Nellie Noland on October 13, indicating how he felt about the general: "Have to talk to God's right hand man tomorrow." The president arrived on October 15. Neither of the principals had ever met. Casually dressed, in an open collar, capped by a greasy hat, the general greeted Truman . Truman took note of his disrespect but said nothing. Averell Harriman, whose plane touched down earliest, tipped Truman's plan to MacArthur by telling him that the group was at Wake Island to discuss a political settlement to the war. Truman told MacArthur that he worried about Chinese intervention, but the general disabused him of the idea and said the war would be over by Thanksgiving, North Korea's capital falling in a week, and by Christmas the US Eighth Army, which was tasked with fighting in Korea, would be back in Japan. The UN would hold elections, and there would be no occupation of Korea and the remaining troops would go home. Other issues were discussed: Formosa and Indochina. Truman gave MacArthur the Distinguished Service Medal and flew home, happy with the conference's work. They had all entered the wonderful world of Oz, MacArthur behind the curtains whirling away at the controls.

Truman learned on November 1 that Chinese Communist soldiers were now fighting UN forces. Then he was pulled in another direction when he was the target of an assassination attempt at Blair House. It was a short, bloody interlude to the problem of Korea. There was no relation, only an attempt by two pro-independence Puerto Rican activists.

The next two months were the darkest period of Truman's presidency. Truman wrote, in drafting a speech on September 1, 1950: "We have met the challenge of the pagan wolves—we shall continue to meet it." The metaphor may have pleased him, but all was not so simple. The November elections were a disappointment, as so many Democrats lost their seats. Democrats still, however, controlled both houses of Congress. The big political worry was Korea. MacArthur was told he could bomb bridges on the Korean side of the Yalu River, which the Chinese were using to cross into Korea, but not to enlarge the war. No air strikes were to be conducted north of the Yalu. MacArthur planned one more powerful punch to end the war, splitting the army into east and west cohorts. It was this disastrous decision that would deny him the victory he sought. A mountain range separated the two UN armies, so neither could come to the aid of the other if something untoward occurred. As it did. At around Thanksgiving the Chinese attacked MacArthur's forces with 260,000 soldiers. Truman had approved crossing the 38th parallel, but he had added precautions that MacArthur threw to the wind. The president had sowed the seed and was now reaping the whirlwind. MacArthur asked for more troops, including those of Formosa's Chiang Kai-shek, a naval blockade of China, and the bombing of the Chinese mainland. The president met with his advisers. Marshall was clear that the country ought not to get into a war with China, and Truman was adamant about not starting a world war, which would be a disaster for humanity. He never admired MacArthur, calling him in a memo in 1945 "a bunco man" and "Mr. Prima Donna, Brass Hat, Five Star MacArthur. He's worse than the Cabots and the Lodges—they at least talked with one another before they told God what to do. Mac tells God right off."

The Chinese hit MacArthur's divided forces—his gamble of splitting his forces had backfired and he was now leading one of the great retreats in history. Was it like Xenophon's retreat of the immortal ten thousand or Napoleon's withdrawal from Moscow? The feisty Captain Truman decided to stay in Korea and told reporters that the United States would fight with every weapon at hand. At a press conference, he misspoke that the commander in the field would have control of the use of the atomic bomb. He quickly corrected himself after a firestorm from friendly countries and reiterated that only the president could authorize the use of atomic weapons. It was a major crisis situation, and all the participants were in crisis mode. MacArthur started to defend himself with public statements, which he had been earlier forbidden to do by the president. The tragedy of the failed UN offensive stunned the military and civilians in charge. Truman later wrote that he probably ought to have relieved MacArthur of his command at this point, but he didn't. There was talk of another Dunkirk, but no new orders were given. It was no longer a dream but a nightmare to try to unite Korea. It would remain divided, and Truman and others decided to seek an armistice at the 38th parallel. The British prime minister, Clement Attlee, was so disturbed by talk of using atomic weapons to reverse the course of events that he rushed to America to confer with Truman and try to get a commitment that no atomic weaponry would be used without consultation. He did not get a pledge. One must recall that the intentions of the Soviet Union, which now had atomic weapons, were unclear. Kennan had warned the State Department, in the Long Telegram in 1946 and the so-called X Article, published in *Foreign Affairs* magazine in 1947, that Russia had never given up its despotic aims and its imperial dreams, which it had held for 300 years. And Stalin had publicly claimed that communism and capitalism were incompatible.

Unfortunately, the internal struggles about the nature and future of communism were being played out not only in Korea and Moscow but also within the country in a Red Scare fomented by Republicans and their allies in the journalistic world and in Congress. Led by one of the nation's great demagogues, Senator Joseph McCarthy, the furor centered about accusations of communists in government, colored all events, and threw the nation into turmoil, pushing aside all the important happenings in foreign and domestic programs. Those attuned to history knew this was one more spasm in American politics that would fade away, but damage was done to reputations and Truman expanded his Loyalty Program, unwisely, to blunt challenges. Many persons were dismissed without full investigations. Reputations were injured and careers ruined before McCarthy overreached, and his personal behavior—heavy drinking, ties to lobbyists, income irregularities, and even sub-rosa intimations of homosexuality among his staff—brought him down. Ever the historian, Truman wrote to friends that he expected the McCarthy business to be put into perspective soon: "I think we have these animals on the run" and "Hysteria strikes this country about once in a generation. . . . It will pass . . . but we must keep our heads and jealously protect those rights which are guaranteed under the Constitution." Truman viewed the Republicans' onslaught as a way for them to end the bipartisan foreign policy forged during World War II, as well as a political ruse to win the next election. In a press conference his anger rose as he said: "To try to sabotage the foreign policy of the United States is just as bad in this cold war as it would be to shoot our soldiers in the back in a hot war." Nevertheless, Congress passed an amendment to the sabotage and espionage laws, over Truman's veto, that was pushed by new legislators who had won office on the Red Scare issue, like Richard Nixon. Truman thought such new men in Washington did not have "the guts of a gnat." A later Senate report concluded that McCarthy didn't prove a single charge of communism against his nemeses. He was a "fraud and a hoax." He ran a campaign of half-truths and untruths. Whether the Red Scare was a more serious rent in the fabric of the nation than the Alien and Sedition Acts passed under John Adams would be a perennial subject for historians to argue over.

Truman took a break from mounting stress and great decisions and took Attlee to a concert by Margaret, who was enjoying a minor career as a singer of light opera and song. She was on a tour and happy in her career, after graduating from college. Truman was inordinately proud of his daughter, who despite the attention children of presidents get, which often injures them, had carved out an independent life. Unfortunately for her, a music critic of a Washington newspaper cut her no slack. He panned her and elicited the worst public letter Truman ever wrote, intemperate and irate, to the music reviewer, writing that he wanted to punch him in the nose and below the belt. It was as though Truman had MacArthur in mind, and exploded with displaced anger. Charlie Ross, his inimitable press secretary and oldest friend, his great emotional balance wheel, had recently died, and so there was no one to stop Truman mailing such a letter. Ross would have had Harry put it in the drawer full of many other such fulminations (most of which have since been published in a volume of unsent letters). Only later did Truman think that perhaps it was not a good idea to attack a music critic. It surely embarrassed his beloved daughter. But this contretemps was only a blip on a screen.

The Korean War relentlessly held Washington's attention. Allied forces retreated 300 miles south, and in about two weeks the UN was out of the North. By the end of the year, Seoul was again in danger. MacArthur radioed about hordes of Chinese, but we now know that the UN forces were never outnumbered. MacArthur's response to the Chinese invasion was the utter destruction of everything between the war front and the Yalu. A swath of destruction, against every village, met Chinese forces right into South Korea. This totality of modern war was evident to American journalists. The US completely devastated the area between the Yalu and the capital of Pyonyang. There were no more cities in the north. Reports were reminiscent of what had happened in some southern cities in the American Civil War, when all houses were destroyed, leaving only chimneys standing like mute soldiers. Nothing was left in Korea but wide mounds of ashes, perversely colored violet. An official history reported: "So, we killed civilians, friendly civilians, and bombed their homes; fired whole villages with the occupants—women and children and ten times as many hidden Communist soldiers—under showers of napalm, and the pilots came back to their ships stinking of vomit twisted up from their vitals by the shock of what they had to do."

MacArthur had wanted, and still asked, to widen the war. He proposed bombing and blockading China and using Chiang Kai-shek's troops. He was denied. He was told that a truce was the best way out, and he was to protect the troops and Japan. Still, he persisted and asked for the atomic bombing of Manchuria and Chinese cities. The Joint Chiefs agreed with him about hitting Chinese cities. But Truman demurred. He would not use atomic weapons against China, or even North Korea, for example, by atomic bombing the large dam on the Yalu River. The president's vivid memories of the horrid conditions of war he had experienced as Captain Truman never left him. He was not a hard-boiled military officer or commander in chief, but a soft-hearted human being doing a tough job with mercy and charity. The president was patient with MacArthur, unlike Acheson, who thought the general disloyal to his commander in chief. Truman increased the defense budget, and Matthew Ridgway, in command of the Eighth Army after its general was killed in a car crash, reported success in January 1951. He became the chief reporter about military conditions, not MacArthur. His offensive retook Seoul. He commanded 365,000 troops against an enemy of 480,000 soldiers but had better artillery and reached the 38th parallel. MacArthur was disheartened because he wanted to unify Korea. MacArthur could not bear to end his career in checkmate. The general never deviated from a position, made privately in March in a letter, then made public in April by Republican Joe Martin on the floor of Congress that "There is no substitute for victory."

The tide turned in the UN's favor by mid-March, and now Truman wanted peace talks with China, which were supported by both the State Department and the military. MacArthur did not agree with the decision to talk to the Chinese and thought

Truman was losing courage. He was particularly incensed that he was denied the tactic of hot pursuit to rout the enemy. Truman ordered a ceasefire proposal to be presented to the UN on behalf of the seventeen nations fighting. There was to be no war with China. Then MacArthur, on his own, and not of the same mind as policy makers in Washington, gave his own ultimatum to China, as well as an invitation to reach a settlement. His actions were outrageous to Acheson and General Omar Bradley, chairman of the Joint Chiefs of Staff. An act of "sabotage," "insubordination," and "unforgivable" were terms bandied about. Acheson and Lovett thought MacArthur ought to be relieved of his command immediately. Truman was furious, he later recorded. In his *Memoirs* he wrote that MacArthur was in defiance of his orders. "This was a challenge to the President under the Constitution.... By this act MacArthur left me no choice— I could no longer tolerate his insubordination." At the very moment, however, he restrained himself and only reminded MacArthur of an order he had issued on December 6, 1950, forbidding the general from making public statements without clearing them first with Washington. While this battle between a general and his commander in chief was going on, UN forces continued to suffer grievous losses, with 228,941 casualties, including 57,120 Americans. This had become a great war.

In conferences with Truman, his unofficial war cabinet clearly indicated that MacArthur had to be relieved of his command. The members were vocal. As with so many of his major decisions, recorded in his diary, Truman wrote that he had made up his mind much before his advisers spoke up. In retrospect, it is hard to know how to weigh such statements, made so often, in judging Truman's leadership. Was he always ahead of his advisers, or was his diary a considered account of how he wished he had acted? At this critical time, Acheson told the president that if he relieved MacArthur he "would have the biggest fight of your administration." On April 9 the Joint Chiefs concluded that MacArthur had to give up his command. The general had a lot of support in Congress among Republicans and was the beneficiary of the ugly Red Scare abroad in the country, yet Truman reported to his war team that he had decided to relieve the five-star general of his duties. In a long walk, Truman shared his decision with two close friends, reminding them that Lincoln had reached such a crossroads when he fired General George B. McClellan, commander of the Army of the Potomac in the Civil War, for not following his orders to go on the offensive and strike General Robert E. Lee's forces. McClellan had a large and magnificent army just sitting in encampments. MacArthur's battlefield situation was different, but the constant was the same: the president was the commander in chief and the general subject to his orders.

There were mixups in transmitting Truman's order to give up his command, and the president was fearful that, because of a leak, MacArthur would resign first and avoid being fired. Truman did not want to give the general the easy way out. He wanted to fire him and uphold a constitutional principle. MacArthur was stunned but saved his vanity by thinking the commander in chief was mentally unstable, had a bad heart, and would soon be dead. But Truman was healthy and clear-headed.

He told the American people in April 1951 that the Korean War was a limited war, he did not intend to start a third world war, and General MacArthur did not agree with him. It was as simple as that. Truman's closest military advisers supported him in congressional hearings on the MacArthur firing. He lost political support with his decision, but it has been generally approved by historians over the years. The Constitution made the president commander in chief, and Truman intended to uphold the Founding Fathers' decision.

On November 30, Truman appeared to rattle the atomic bomb to stop the Chinese in Korea with some ill-chosen words at a press conference. He did not mean to and pulled back quickly. Luckily, the Soviet Union was not willing to contemplate a world war over Korea, and the Chinese seemed to indicate that it only wanted to fight to secure the 38th parallel. Ridgway saved Seoul, with heavy fighting, and the American forces crossed the 38th parallel. In late spring 1951, the fighting stabilized. Even though two more years of heavy fighting ensued, without significant territorial change, peace negotiations were under way, lasting two years. Truman agreed to the proposed ceasefire. He thought he might be faced with another decision to use the atomic bomb, this time to rescue American troops from being annihilated. The game changer, however, was that now Russia had the bomb and looked after its Chinese ally with greater interest. But it was President Eisenhower, Truman's successor, who got South Korea to accept the old division of Korea, in exchange for significant aid and a defense treaty. South Korea's president never signed the armistice. The story of Eisenhower's own saber rattling and the tortuous issues leading to an end to the war are subjects for a different book, beyond Truman's presidency.

Today, about 30,000 troops remain in Korea as a tripwire in any war against South Korea, now a booming economy and an adequate democracy. Truman's gift to the American people was less the containment of communism in Korea than the bolstering of the constitutional mandate that the president was commander in chief of the nation's armed forces. There would be no man on horseback, as France too often had suffered from. In this episode in his life, Truman was an embodiment of George Washington in his courage. The first president actually headed up an army to put down a rebellion over liquor taxes. Truman could not foresee that in future years his constitutional gift would be abused by future presidents. New wars were fought without any congressional declaration of war, but only by actions of the president—the Vietnam and the Iraq wars being two conspicuous examples. Meantime, MacArthur came home to great celebrations and congressional hearings. He addressed Congress, saying, among many things, "Old soldiers never die; they just fade away." After a brief flirtation with running for the presidency, he did indeed fade away.

The Korean War—Truman's War in the Age of Acheson— became America's forgotten war. Forgotten, too, was the lesson about the perils of sending an American army to fight in Asia or, indeed, on any large land mass of an unknown national culture. Korea was at the apex of the Cold War. Truman militarized the containment policy of hemming in communism by economic and diplomatic means, not understanding, or wantonly misunderstanding, George Kennan's policy recommendation. Kennan had urged peaceful competition, not war and, as the architect of containment, was thought to be against the Korean War. American hubris began on the shores of Korea and has not diminished with the years. Truman learned the wrong history lessons from World War I and its aftermath. There were limits to military power in strange lands against multitudes of soldiers from little-known cultures. What might have worked in a European context did not apply to Asia or the Middle East. What Truman did keep that was valuable was his courage and leadership, the first never doubted, the second supported by strong-minded advisers. The Korean War transformed the United States into a very different country. It soon had hundreds of permanent military bases abroad, a large standing army, and a permanent national security state at home. We can add to that a huge nuclear force, a penchant for invading foreign countries on little, or no, evidence of danger to the US, and a government not always protective of civil liberties.

Aside from the nightmarish war, 1951 was a year of some accomplishments for Truman. He told Prime Minister Attlee that he was not going to give up on Asia and save Europe only, as Attlee, who had flown to Washington in some distress, wanted. Truman took the whole world as his workshop. A final peace treaty with Japan, defense treaties with the Philippines and ANZUS (Australia, New Zealand, the US), an alliance with Nationalist China on Formosa, and one with South Korea were signed. A joint committee of Congress looked into MacArthur's firing. But all was put to rest when General Omar Bradley voiced his judgment that a war with China would be "the wrong war, in the wrong place, at the wrong time, with the wrong enemy." The drums of the pro–Chiang Kai-shek China lobby beating for war with Communist China stilled for a while.

Truman recorded that he "never worked so hard on a speech" as his State of the Union Address in 1951. As he looked back, his accomplishments were, indeed, in the foreign policy field and hardly noticed by Americans, who were still catching up after wartime deprivations. His domestic program in 1949 had had only one major achievement, a housing bill. Among the provisions in the bill were those for public housing, which a generation later because of poor, or no, maintenance, would become slums. Only years later did policy makers realize that the poor needed more than better housing but also better health care and education. But a recession had begun. It was a perilous time for any ambitious programs. Wartime conditions took over budgets and attention. But this year, Truman had changed economic advisers, and an emphasis was put on economic growth and not redistribution, the latter an inheritance from the New Deal. The change fueled good economic times. Truman had determined to make the Democratic Party a Farmer-Labor organization, following up on his 1948 victory. He had talked of progressive liberalism, a description that, in retrospect, made no sense. He was linking Theodore Roosevelt and Franklin Roosevelt, making a kind of two-cousin label. But the budding alliance between Southern Democrats and Republicans was blossoming into a thorny hedge blocking large initiatives. The domestic program trumpeted in his 1949 State of the Union Address was not well received. Taft-Hartley was not repealed; there were no new Tennessee Valley Authority–type programs; there was no medical insurance, no federal aid to education, no immigration or real civil rights reform, some aid to farmers, some reclamation projects and additional public electric power. There was a raise in the minimum wage, and some reform in Social Security. Controls on the economy remained a problem; there were no new taxes, and a balanced budget was elusive. Truman vetoed a natural gas bill that decontrolled prices. Truman's domestic program was a combination of small triumphs, not a super program to give Truman a great reputation as a domestic leader. It was a program of special interests at work, and working together, to satisfy constituents and advance reelection prospects. Truman had not labeled his domestic program and only talked of giving the people a fair deal, as Franklin Roosevelt had given in a New Deal and, before him, Theodore Roosevelt in a Square Deal. It was the journalists who labeled his policies a Fair Deal. Truman liked the label and began using it. But it was never a program that emerged full blown from his head in a systematic way. He always thought he was extending the New Deal of a successful and esteemed predecessor.

The last years were marked by scandals of corrupt officials and investigations. At first, Truman did not react quickly or well. He was lulled into his old Pendergast mode: I am honest; the other fellows are not. He did clean up an enormous scandal in the Reconstruction Finance Corporation (which provided funds to rebuild the country during the depression and war), with firings and criminal indictments, but that good deed was accomplished in the time of the burning Korean War, and was lost in the headlines. Tennessee Democratic Senator Estes Kefauver led a committee to investigate crime in the nation, with a keen eye on Kansas City, which angered Truman. Kefauver was relentless, while opening up on the possibility of running for president. He found no links to Truman. But all was not over for the besieged president. Scandals erupted in the Bureau of Internal Revenue (now called the Internal Revenue Service) and the Tax Division of the Justice Department. Once more, Truman did not jump quickly on the matter. After months of investigation, fifty-seven crooked IRS workers were fired. Not until January 1952 did Truman reorganize the tax bureau and bring in the civil service to make the organization honest. Truman's attorney general was not up to the job of cleaning house but would not leave. He finally did, but his replacement was not a strong official. A problem was that Truman thought scandals would inevitably occur when huge sums of money were available. He had been through all this in Missouri. Some things never changed.

Truman looked back on both the 80th and 81st Congresses in diary entries. At first, because of foreign policy wins, he called the 80th Congress "one hell of a session." That was when Republicans had roared back, incredibly hostile to him. His view soon faded on reflection, as he faced its successor in 1949, a Democratic Congress. He penned:

> Trying to make the 81st Congress perform is and has been worse than cussing the 80th. A President never loses prestige

fighting Congress. And I can't fight my own Congress. There are some terrible chairmen in the 81st. But so far things have come out *fairly* well. I've kissed and petted more consarned S.O.B. so-called Democrats and left wing Republicans [than] all the Presidents put together. I have very few people fighting my battles in Congress as I [when a senator] fought F.D.R's.

It would seem that Truman was hatching, perhaps not entirely consciously, a political plan for the future: his enemies would not be Republican presidential candidates but recalcitrant Congresses, whether Democratic in alliance with Southern refuseniks or Republicans in a majority.

This dark episode in Truman's presidency may have had at its root the way in which the Democratic Party was changing. For example, there was an emerging middle class that did not want, or like, political machines. It was more sophisticated, better educated, and thought for itself. Truman did not understand the new base of the Democratic Party and what leadership demanded. The president needed to define the agenda of political debate, set a tone for the people, and craft an eloquently phrased vision. In American politics, when this was not done, as it was by Jefferson, Lincoln, and the two Roosevelts, for example, a military figure captured the country, for example, Jackson, Zachary Taylor, and Eisenhower.

The last year of Truman's presidency was marred by the threat of a steel strike. Steel was the basic industry in the country. It affected peacetime activity and wartime needs, that is, in this instance, needs of the Korean War. Because no contract had been negotiated after 99 days, Truman nationalized the mills.

It was a gamble, just as going into Korea and devising the Inchon landing were. Commerce Secretary Charles Sawyer was not strong enough to convince mill owners to accept a government settlement, and Truman once more lost his temper about the head of the major mill: "I want you to fire that son of a bitch right away and put a general in charge of running the mills." Sawyer had no such power, Truman calmed down, and the American people were divided on the seizure, though more were opposed than supported it; in one poll, 35 percent were for it, 43 percent against. The Supreme Court ruled the seizure illegal, six to two. It did not like the imputation of inherent power of the president, preferred that Taft-Hartley be invoked, and since the Korean War was never a declared war, it could not be a reason for action. A long strike ensued until Truman brought the parties together with terms that had been offered months before: a raise for workers, formal recognition of a union shop, and a rise in the price of steel. Truman did not forgive the liberals, on and off the Court, who did not stand with him. He thought the Court decision "crazy." There was a war on. And he never developed the elegant speaking skills to woo Americans and influentials. His charisma was earthy. Things that Roosevelt could get away with, he could not. But one ought not to rule out poor judgment on the steel seizure.

Truman would not run again. He was tempted to stay and defend himself and his record, but his first instincts took hold. His staff was told of his decision twice in 1951. The president canvassed a variety of possible men to succeed him, including Eisenhower, but settled on the eloquent and elegant Adlai

Stevenson, governor of Illinois. Then he unwisely let his own name be entered in the New Hampshire primary, and Kefauver beat him. Truman succeeded in baffling those closest to him about his plans, except Bess, who just told him he ought not to run and she could not take another term in the White House. His closest friends then talked to him and mentioned his age—sixty-eight—as a prime factor in retiring. Truman waited until the March 1952 Jefferson-Jackson Day Dinner in Washington, DC, to announce he was retiring. Bess "looked the way you do when you draw four aces," Harry Vaughan recalled. Truman thought he might rejoin the Senate, but he would not seek the post. The idea quickly died because Bess only wanted to go home. Once more it was clear that she never liked Washington that much. Once the cave dwellers had declared that wearing seersucker dresses in the summer in Washington was not acceptable for a First Lady, she had wanted out as soon as practical.

Stevenson finally decided to run for president. His constituency was an educated middle class who almost fawned over his intellect, charisma, rhetoric, and presence. Could he be another Roosevelt? The Republicans nominated Eisenhower, another war hero and general for a party long out of power and itching to get back the highest office in the land. Eisenhower had changed his mind when the Korean War kept on killing boys and there seemed no end to it. He was approached by Republican elders who told him that only he could save the country and party. (He had declared he was a Republican late in the game.) Eisenhower promised to end the Korean War, Stevenson was saddled with Truman's scandals, and too many Democrats liked Ike. It was a personal victory for the hero of Word War II because little was known of his politics or ideas. Eisenhower had long coattails, and Congress went Republican. The great era of Franklin Roosevelt and Harry Truman was over. The country was prosperous and secure, but that was not enough to elect a Democratic president. There was a feeling that change was needed. The long Democratic ascendancy was not good for the country. The change was not cataclysmic, much as Republicans hoped it would be, for the age of reform was securely in place. At this juncture, another change took place in the Trumans' lives, when Madge Gates Wallace, "Mr. Truman's" mother-in-law, died in Washington.

Truman met with Eisenhower, and aides on both sides discussed the presidency. It set a standard for future transitions. He gave a Farewell Address. On Inauguration Day, Eisenhower refused to enter the White House to join the outgoing president for coffee and chitchat but waited for Truman to join him in his car, a gross disrespect. Acheson gave the Trumans, cabinet members, and close friends lunch at his Georgetown residence. The family left Washington on the magnificent *Ferdinand Magellan,* with crowds cheering. They arrived in Independence to more crowds and to their house with more people greeting them. Their many affectionate sendoffs made for a happy ending. The Trumans were home alone and to the very first house of their own. The man of Middle America had been at the center of momentous national and international events for so long. Now, when asked what he had done when he got home, he jauntily

FIGURE 21 The home of President Harry S. Truman, 219 N. Delaware, Independence, Missouri, in the winter, ca. 1947. *Credit:* Vernon Galloway, courtesy of the Harry S. Truman Library.

and characteristically ended his public life with these laconic words about suitcases: "I took the grips up to the attic." While president, Truman had placed on his desk a sign that said: "The buck stops here." But he really preferred the saying he had found on a cross over a cowboy's grave in Tombstone, Arizona: "He done his damnedest."

POSTSCRIPT

Harry Truman lived until age eighty-eight and died in 1972 of old age. Bess had him buried in the courtyard of the Truman Library after an Episcopalian service, which was also attended by a Baptist minister—Harry had joined that church as a young man, it should be recalled—and a Masonic leader. She covered all the bases. An honor guard fired a salute, and she received an American flag. Bess had approved the epitaph for Harry's tombstone, which he had written. It contained his birth and death dates, Margaret's birth date, and all his public offices with dates. Ten years later Bess too was buried in the courtyard, her tombstone merely stating: "First Lady of the United States, 1945–1953."

Truman's last years were happy and eventful. The first thing he did was to buy a new black Chrysler V-8 sedan, 4,300 pounds, with power steering and power brakes to take Bess on a trip across country to the East, unfettered by Secret Service agents. They just wanted to be two plain American citizens, staying at all kinds of hotels and eating at various ordinary places. Not too often they were recognized. They were carefree for the first time since 1945. Truman wanted to become Mr. Citizen after being Mr. President. Harry always loved to drive, and Bess was his best companion, as long as he drove only fifty miles an hour, she believing he always drove too fast. He mapped out the trip like an old soldier planning a campaign, and they rambled through Missouri, and then Illinois, Indiana, Ohio, West Virginia, Virginia, Pennsylvania, New York, New Jersey, Maryland, and Washington, DC. The exact itinerary is less important here than their daring journey over sometimes poor roads, highways with bad drivers, towns of poor accommodations, and often incomplete maps.

He then planned to write his memoirs. Doubleday gave him an extraordinary advance of $600,000, at a time when the average working man earned $4,000 a year. He put together a research and writing team to help him, but it was so expensive, he claimed he only cleared $37,000 from the two-volume publication in 1955. He entitled the work *Memoirs of Harry S. Truman.* Volume 1 carried the subtitle *1945: Year of Decisions,* and Volume 2, *1946–52: Years of Trial and Hope.* The work was not a success because Truman prepared such a long and unorganized manuscript that when an editor was called in to shape it, the task proved overwhelming. The tomes were not insightful or reflective of Truman's remarkable life and work. His voice was missing.

Truman also was busy building a library and research center to house his voluminous papers, organize educational programs, and give him an office. He could, eventually, walk from his house to the new building. He loved talking to children who visited the place, although by now his memory of events was often skewed. No matter. The children loved the grandfatherly ex-president. Margaret and her husband, Clifton Daniel, and their four boys visited the Trumans during these last years, to the delight of both grandparents.

Truman didn't think much of the Eisenhower presidency, but seldom spoke out. Rather, he thought about what he had contributed to the country's benefit. It is an exercise worth exploring even now.

He never wanted to be president and truly enjoyed being a senator, which he hoped to be for two or three terms only. He took on the job of president without training or experience, and worked like a Trojan to master it. His domestic policies were mostly derivative. He had some of Teddy Roosevelt's western progressivism and Franklin Roosevelt's New Deal liberalism. But unlike them he had minimal success in achieving big domestic victories. Rather, his achievements fell in the fields of diplomacy and wartime leadership.

Truman, like Washington, Lincoln, and Wilson, served in the highest office at a time of winning wars and reconstructing countries in peacetime. Washington succeeded brilliantly, winning a revolution, serving as the first president of a new kind of government, a democracy, and presiding over the writing of a constitution that is the most lasting in world history. Lincoln won a war to save the Union and free four million slaves. But he was assassinated before he could reconstruct the country, and it went in a direction probably different from what he could have managed. What he could have achieved with his brilliant leadership was not to be. The Congress led with radical means—a military ascendancy over southern, rebellious states—to get to needed and essential ends, that is, the protection of the victory that was so dearly won to keep the country united and assistance to the freed slaves to live like other Americans, with all their rights. Wilson helped win a fiercely fought world war and write peace terms to turn the adversaries of the Allies into peaceful nations, but could not get the US Senate to approve the keystone of the arch of victory, the League of Nations. Then he had a stroke that ended his leadership.

Only Truman ended wars and oversaw the peace of the world, with a United Nations to maintain the peace in the future. That he could not get the Soviet Union to join in the endeavor is the great pity of this second world conflict. But his achievement of standing at the bridge to protect democracies and thwart communist takeovers is massive. He put Europe together and protected it, fed the hungry, and encouraged industry and agriculture. Europe was remade. In Asia he was less successful, as he too hastily went to war over Korea and could not end it before leaving office. It was the great tragedy of his presidency. His instincts for collective security, however, were true, and the diplomacy of alliances held communism at bay in that great land mass. Truman could inspire good men to join him in government, although his tenderness for old friends around him stained his reputation when they engaged in corrupt practices. But he was always personally honest. It was part of the greatness of the country that a man like Truman, indeed

like Lincoln, could rise from humble beginnings, educate himself, and lead a great country to do great things. In Truman's
case, coming out of a political system in his early years of widespread corruption is something of an American story of re-
demption. That at the end, he did not understand the changing
nature of the Democratic Party, now driven by an educated
middle class that would not tolerate old, fraudulent, ways of
winning elections, was disappointing. When all these elements
in Truman's career are weighed, he comes out not as a Mount
Rushmore great president but rather a triumphant near-great
president. And in the pantheon of presidents since Washington,
this is a tribute few others have achieved.

ACKNOWLEDGMENTS

I owe many debts to those who over the past few years have helped me write this book or cheered me on. Lara Heimert, publisher of Basic Books and friend for many years, enthusiastically acquired the book for Basic, read a draft, and made significant suggestions to strengthen and present it. I am very grateful for her care and interest. Katy O'Donnell, editorial assistant to Lara, helped me in ways too numerous to mention. My agent, Sandy Dijkstra, a friend for over thirty years, eagerly agreed to represent me, again. Her assistant, Elise Capron, was always helpful. I owe Elisabeth James thanks for her contractual skills. Andrew John Kinney was masterful as my liaison, researcher, and editor with the Harry S. Truman Library in Independence, Missouri. Janice Davis at the library was especially helpful in tracking down illustrations with Andrew. I want to thank the librarians at the Truman Library for their quick and expert handling of requests for primary materials on Truman's life and career. Buck Creel, friend and retired army officer, keenly read Chapter 2 and made suggestions. My copyeditor, Norman MacAfee, is peerless in the field. I owe him a great debt for his intense interest and superb editorial skills. Thanks go as well to project editor Sandra Beris, proofreader Anna Kaltenbach, and indexer Douglas Easton.

My family—Bruce, Jenni, Aleta, and Maia—were always enthusiastic supporters. Many friends deserve mention for their interest, for many years, about this book. They include Catherine Clinton, Mickey and Phyllis Keller, David and Sonia Landes, Susan Wallace Boehmer, Sylvia Mendenhall, Ellen Fitzpatrick, Dan Kevles, Dr. Vivian Sanchez, Dan and Linda Pessoni, Steve and Sheila Zager, David and Lee Duff, and Kristi Stone.

　　This book is dedicated to Kathleen Nichols, my friend who got me back to work after I put the book aside for a year, distraught over the death of my husband, David Herbert Donald, in 2009. My great champion, he had read only one chapter. No words can express my great thanks to Kathleen for getting my life back on track as a person and a writer.

SELECT BIBLIOGRAPHY

There is an enormous literature on Harry Truman's life and career. I have read most of it, and have profited by it in crafting this short life. I have selected the books and articles that I found most helpful and note them here below. I am aware of the historical disputes about Truman's life and decisions and, after deep considerations, offer my own determinations.

Every chapter in this book has benefited from two superb biographies of Harry S. Truman: David McCullough, *Truman*, New York, 1992, and Alonzo L. Hamby, *A Man of the People: A Life of Harry S. Truman*, New York, 1995. They do not always agree on key issues, to the benefit of a new biographer seeking her own interpretation. But there is no gainsaying the immense and deep research embedded in each book. We who write about Truman stand on the shoulders of these two giants. I suggest to my readers that they peruse each author's bibliography for complete sources for Truman's life.

In their biographies, both McCullough and Hamby give us the wide and deep sources in manuscript collections, personal interviews, oral histories, and newspapers. Their books, and my own, here, are the benefits of their research. Often, I cite such sources in the text of my book, especially newspapers, but, mostly, I silently rely on their sources, especially when they agree, for ordinary information. Because this book is intended for the busy, general reader, I have not annotated it, as I would a path-breaking work. But my manuscript draft is fully annotated as to the sources I used.

The following are lists of books and articles that I found most helpful and I collected in my small Truman library. Some can be found on the Internet, and I so cite them for the reader. The following are both primary and secondary sources.

Algeo, Matthew, *Harry Truman's Excellent Adventure,* Chicago, 2009.

Alperovitz, Gar, *Atomic Diplomacy: Hiroshima and Potsdam,* New York, 1965.

Atomic Bomb Decisions. Timetable with Explanations, May 10–August 9, 1945, from U.S. National Archives, http://www.dannen.com/

The Avalon Project, *The Atomic Bombings of Hiroshima and Nagasaki,* Chapter 3, Summary of Damages; Chapter 4, Main Conclusions; Chapter 6, Descriptions of Cities Before Bombing. Yale Law School Library, The Avalon Project. The most interesting conclusion is the underestimation of radiation damage, long range. http://avalon.law.yale.edu/subject_menus/mpmenu.asp

Bernstein, Barton J., and Allen J. Matusow, editors, *The Truman Administration: A Documentary History,* New York, 1966.

Bix, Herbert P., "Why Did the Japanese Delay Surrendering?" George Mason University, History News Network. The role of the emperor is discussed. http://hnn.us/articles/12947.html

Burnes, Brian, *Harry S. Truman: His Life and Times,* Kansas City, Missouri, 2003.

Butow, Robert, *Japan's Decision to Surrender,* Palo Alto, California, 1954.

Costigliola, Frank, *Roosevelt's Lost Alliances: How Personal Politics Helped Start the Cold War,* Princeton, 2011.

Cummings, Bruce, *The Korean War: A History,* New York, 2010.

Dallek, Robert, *Hail to the Chief: The Making and Unmaking of American Presidents,* New York, 1996.

Dallek, Robert, *Harry S. Truman,* New York, 2008.

Daniel, Clifton Truman, *Dear Harry, Love Bess: Bess Truman's Letters to Harry Truman, 1919–1943,* Kirksville, Missouri, 2011. This book came out after I completed my book. It is a wonderful compilation of lost letters that show that the Truman marriage was a love match and Bess was apprised of many of Truman's endeavors and gave advice.

Daniels, Jonathan, *The Man of Independence*, Philadelphia, 1950.

Daniels, Roger, editor, *Immigration and the Legacy of Harry S. Truman*, Kirksville, Missouri, 2010.

"The Decision to Drop the Atomic Bomb," Online Research File, Truman Library. March 1945–August 1963. http://www.trumanlibrary.org/whistlestop/study_collections/bomb/large/index.php

Donovan, Robert J., *Conflict and Crisis: The Presidency of Harry S. Truman, 1945–1948*, New York, 1977.

Donovan, Robert J., *Tumultuous Years: The Presidency of Harry S. Truman, 1949–1953*, New York, 1982.

Dorset, Lyle W., *The Pendergast Machine*, New York, 1968.

Ferrell, Robert H., editor, *The Autobiography of Harry S. Truman*, Columbia, Missouri, 1980, 2002.

Ferrell, Robert H., editor, *Dear Bess: The Letters from Harry to Bess Truman, 1910–1959*, New York, 1983.

Ferrell, Robert H., *Harry S. Truman and the Modern Presidency*, New York, 1983.

Ferrell, Robert H., *Harry S. Truman: A Life*, Columbia, Missouri, 1994.

Ferrell, Robert H., editor, *Off the Record: The Private Papers of Harry S. Truman*, Columbia, Missouri, 1980.

Ferrell, Robert H., *Truman & Pendergast*, Columbia, Missouri, 1999.

Ferrell, Robert H., editor, *Truman and the Bomb: A Documentary History, Recommended Readings*, Harry S. Truman Library and Museum, http://www.trumanlibrary.org/whistlestop/study_collections/bomb/large/index.php?action=lessons

Fisk, Bret, and Cary Karakas, *The Firebombing of Tokyo and Its Legacy*. US bombs killed 187,000 Japanese, etc. Special Issue of *The Asia-Pacific Journal*, edited by Fisk and Karacas, http://japanfocus.org/-Bret-Fisk/3469

Frank, Richard B., Review of *Hiroshima in History: The Myths of Revisionism*, ed. Robert James Maddox, George Mason University,

History News Network, 8-22-07, http://hnn.us/roundup/entries /42108.html

Gaddis, John Lewis, *The Cold War: A New History*, New York, 2007.

Gardner, Michael R., *Harry Truman and Civil Rights: Moral Courage and Political Risks*, Carbondale, Illinois, 2002.

Geselbracht, Ray, and David C. Acheson, editors, *Affection and Trust: The Personal Correspondence of Harry S. Truman and Dean Acheson, 1953–1971*, New York, 2010.

Giangreco, D. M., *Hell to Pay: Operation DOWNFALL and the Invasion of Japan, 1945–1947*, Annapolis, 2009.

Giangreco, D. M., *The Soldier from Independence: A Military Biography of Harry Truman*, Minneapolis, 2009.

Greenfield, Kent Roberts, *Command Decision*, New York, 1959.

Gruhl, Werner, "It's Time to Acknowledge That Hiroshima Followed Imperial Japan's Decision to Launch a Terrible War Against Its Neighbors," George Mason University, History News Network, 12-02-07, http://hnn.us/articles/44729.html

Halberstam, David, *The Coldest Winter: America and the Korean War*, New York, 2007.

Hamby, Alonzo L. *Beyond the New Deal: Harry S. Truman and American Liberalism*, New York, 1973.

Hamby, Alonzo L., *Man of the People: A Life of Harry S. Truman*, New York, 1995.

Hasegawa, Tsuyoshi, *Racing the Enemy: Stalin, Truman, and the Surrender of Japan*, Cambridge, Massachusetts, 2005.

Hastings, Max, *The Korean War*, New York, 1987.

Hayde, Frank R., *The Mafia and the Machine: The Story of the Kansas City Mob*, Fort Lee, New Jersey, 2007.

"Hiroshima: What People Think Now," Internet Symposium of more than a score of key articles of significance by major scholars, 08-12-10. George Mason University, History News Network, http://hnn.us/articles/10168.html

Interim Committee, Notes of Meetings, May–July, 1945, of the Scientific Panel, to discuss technical and political matters of the atomic bomb, Miscellaneous Historical Documents Collection, Truman Library, http://www.trumanlibrary.org/whistlestop/study _collections/bomb/large/index.php

Karabell, Zachary, *The Last Campaign: How Harry Truman Won the 1948 Election,* New York, 2001.

Keegan, John, *The First World War,* New York, 1998.

Kennedy, David, "Why U.S. Leaders Never Questioned the Idea of Dropping the Bomb," George Mason University, History News Network, 7-25-05, http://hnn.us/roundup/entries/13429.html

Kimura, Motoharu, with John Carpenter, *Living with Nuclei: 50 Years in the Nuclear Age, Memoirs of a Japanese Physicist,* Tokyo, 1990.

Larson, Lawrence H., and Nancy J. Hulson, *Pendergast,* Columbia, Missouri, 1997.

Lawson, Steven F., editor, *To Secure These Rights: The Report of President Harry S. Truman's Committee on Civil Rights,* New York, 2004.

Leuchtenburg, William E., *The White House Looks South: Franklin D. Roosevelt, Harry S. Truman, Lyndon B. Johnson,* Baton Rouge, 2005.

Maddox, Robert James, editor, *Hiroshima in History: The Myths of Revisionism,* Columbia, Missouri, 2007.

Maddox, Robert James, "Why Another Book on Hiroshima?" George Mason University, History News Network, 5-16-07, http://hnn.us/articles/38637.html

Malloy, Sean L., *Atomic Tragedy: Henry L. Stimson and the Decision to Use the Bomb Against Japan,* Ithaca, New York, 2008.

Malloy, Sean L., "Four Days in May . . . Henry Stimson and the Decision to Use the Atomic Bomb," *Asia-Pacific Journal,* 4-4-09. http://japanfocus.org/-Sean-Malloy/3114

McCoy, Donald R., *The Presidency of Harry S. Truman,* Lawrence, Kansas, 1984.

McCullough, David, *Truman,* New York, 1992.

McLaughlin, John J., "The Bomb Was Not Necessary," George Mason University, History News Network, 08-10-10: Japanese peace feelers, surmises, leaks—all rejected as inauthentic: http://hnn.us/articles/129964.html

Moskin, J. Robert, *Mr. Truman's War: The Final Victories of World War II and the Birth of the Postwar World,* New York, 1996.

National Security Archive, *The Atomic Bomb and the End of World War II: A Collection of Primary Sources.* Electronic Briefing Book No. 162. William Burr, editor, Posted 2005, Updated 2007. An essential source. http://www.gwu.edu/~nsarchiv/NSAEBB/NSAEBB162/index.htm

Official Bombing Order, July 25, 1945. U.S. National Archives, Record Group 77. There was no mention of targeting the military or sparing civilians. The cities were the targets. Additional bombs could be dropped when ready. Truman and Stimson approved this order by General Groves. http://www.dannen.com/decision/handy.html

Parrish, Thomas, *Berlin in the Balance: The Blockade, the Airlift, the First Major Battle of the Cold War,* Reading, Massachusetts, 1998.

Pearlman, Michael, *Truman & MacArthur: Policy, Politics, and the Hunger for Honor and Renown,* Bloomington, Indiana, 2008.

Pietrusza, David, *1948: Harry Truman's Improbable Victory and the Year That Transformed America's Role in the World,* New York, 2011.

Poen, Monte M., editor, *Strictly Personal and Confidential: The Letters Harry Truman Never Mailed,* Boston, 1982.

President's Secretary's Files, Truman Library and Internet. Valuable sources from those in White House, Reminiscences, Truman Letters, Conversations, Memoranda of Various Officials. Some are also found in Miscellaneous Historical Documents Collection, 1945–1953, http://www.trumanlibrary.org/hstpaper/psf.htm

Rhodes, Richard, *Dark Sun: The Making of the Hydrogen Bomb,* New York, 1995.

Riddle, Donald, *The Truman Committee: A Study in Congressional Responsibility,* New Brunswick, New Jersey, 1964.

Sherwin, Martin, *A World Destroyed: The Atomic Bomb and the Grand Alliance,* New York, 1975.

Steinberg, Alfred, "How Harry Truman Does His Job," *Saturday Evening Post,* March 3, 1951.

Target Committee Minutes, Second Meeting, Top Secret, Los Alamos, May 10–11, 1945. Re: Decisions on how to drop the bomb to greatest advantage. http://www.dannen.com/decision/targets .html

Troy, Gil, *Mr. and Mrs. President: From the Trumans to the Clintons,* Lawrence, Kansas, 2000, revised edition of *Affairs of State,* New York, 1997.

Truman, Harry S., *Mr. Citizen,* New York, 1953, 1957, 1959, 1960.

Truman, Harry, Diary and Papers re: atomic bombing of Japan, April 12, 1945 to August 14, 1945, http://www.trumanlibrary.org /whistlestop/study_collections/bomb/large/index.php

Truman, Harry S., *Memoirs by Harry S. Truman: Vol. 1: 1945: Year of Decisions; Vol. 2: 1946–52: Years of Trial and Hope,* New York, 1955, 1956.

Truman, Harry S., Harry S. Truman Library, Independence, Missouri: Presidential Papers, two CD-ROMs; World War II FDR, Truman, Churchill, Stalin Conference Documents, one CD-ROM.

[Truman, Harry S.], Printed Documents, Harry S. Truman, *Public Messages, Speeches, Statements, 1945–1953,* 8 Vols., Washington, DC, 1961–1966.

[Truman, Harry S.], *Results of County Planning, Jackson County,* Missouri, no date.

Truman, Margaret, *Harry S. Truman,* New York, 1973.

Truman, Margaret, editor, *Where the Buck Stops: The Personal and Private Writings of Harry S. Truman,* New York, 1989.

"United States Strategic Bombing Survey: The Effects of the Atomic Bombs on Hiroshima and Nagasaki, June 30, 1946," confidential file, Truman Papers, Truman Library, http://www.truman library.org/whistlestop/study_collections/bomb/large/documents /index.php?documentdate=1946-06-30&documentid=7-1&study collectionid=&pagenumber=1

Walker, J. Samuel, *Prompt and Utter Destruction: Truman and the Use of the Atomic Bombs Against Japan,* revised edition, Chapel Hill, North Carolina, 2004.

INDEX